SUCCESS

WITH

PEOPLE

A Simple Six Step Plan That Works

Published by:
    The Napoleon Hill Foundation
    P. O. Box 1277
    Wise, Virginia 24293

    Website: www.naphill.org
    email: napoleonhill@uvawise.edu

Distributed by:
    Kat Ranch Publishing
    140 S. Main Street
    Brooksville, FL 34601
    813-376-8966

ISBN: 978-0-9830008-8-4

What others say about *Success With People* and author Cavett Robert:

"*Success With People* is a book for the ages. Cavett Robert writes for heart, he educates, motivates and inspires. When you finish reading this book, you will understand how his wisdom, warmth and humor impacted millions."

> Charles "Tremendous" Jones, CPAE
> Speaker Hall of Fame

"Always I remember Cavett Robert as being 'front row center'! He was in that special place in every audience, board meeting, or event where I was privileged speaker, participant, or member. A profound visionary, encourager, friend, and consummate professional speaker, Cavett came alongside me (as he did scores of other speakers) with the awe, respect, challenge and encouragement to become all we were meant to be. I have no doubt he is 'front row center' in the 'Heavenly Grandstands' cheering us on . . . even now!"

> Naomi Rhode, CSP, CPAE, Speaker Hall of Fame
> Recipient of Cavett Award

"Cavett Robert is one who stands out in the minds and hearts of thousands of people as an honest giver who asked for nothing back. A person who would get excited about whatever little talent that you had that could mushroom into something that would change your life and the lives of other people. Any work about Cavett Robert and his life and commitment is a great read for anyone no matter who they are, what they are doing or what their life passion is."

> Thom Winninger, CPAE, Speaker Hall of Fame
> Recipient of Cavett Award

"Cavett wrote and spoke in a way that every person can find a connection to their own lives. He was the most encouraging individual anyone ever encountered. When you read this book, he will be a part of your success with people."

Patricia Fripp, CSP, CPAE
Recipient of Cavett Award

"Cavett Robert originated the idea of the National Speakers Association and was a founder, along with a number of other speakers. If you had the privilege of knowing, working with, or hearing him, you know he was a man who inspired all of us. I am grateful I knew Cavett. Early in my speaking career when I had the privilege of speaking on the platform with him, he encouraged me often to write a book. He assured me I had something to say and knew how to say it and that it would benefit others. With his encouragement, I wrote *See You at the Top*, which has now been published in hardback for over 30 years. I believe you would do well to read his book and follow through on what he has to say. This special edition will be a keepsake for you for the rest of your life. Not only that, it will improve the life you now live. Take advantage of it—it's a rare opportunity."

Zig Ziglar, CPAE, Speaker Hall of Fame
Recipient of Cavett Award

SUCCESS
WITH
PEOPLE

A Simple Six Step Plan That Works

By
Cavett Robert

Introduction by
DON M. GREEN
Executive Director
Napoleon Hill Foundation

Published by:
    The Napoleon Hill Foundation
    P. O. Box 1277
    Wise, Virginia 24293

    Website: www.naphill.org
    email: napoleonhill@uvawise.edu

Distributed by:
    Executive Books
    206 W. Allen Street
    Mechanicsburg, PA 17055

    Telephone: 800-233-2665
    Website: www.executivebooks.com

Paperback:
ISBN-13: 978-1-933715-10-0
ISBN-10: 1-933715-10-3

Hardback:
ISBN-13: 978-1-933715-12-4
ISBN-10: 1-933715-12-X

Table of Contents

3. PEOPLE ARE PERSUADED NOT BY WHAT WE SAY BUT BY WHAT THEY UNDERSTAND 45

4. HOW DOES IT BENEFIT ME—NOT YOU, BUT ME? 55

INTRODUCTION

The author will show you that your success in life will be determined by your ability to get along with other people.

By reading Cavett Robert's book, you can become part of the small, fabulously successful group that is responsible for the overwhelming majority of the positive results in the world today.

Human Engineering can be defined as the science of knowing how to deal with people.

Your personal success as well as your financial success is measured by your ability to get along with people. The lesson of human motivation will help you in your determination to meet your goals in life.

This book will show you the proper steps in managing people and how to make them respond to your wishes. One of the important lessons in life is discovering how to sell yourself to others, and get them to help you in anything you may want to attempt.

Follow the six principles in Cavett Robert's book and you can have more money and personal power than you ever dreamed possible.

Principle #1 – Shows you how to cause things to happen and guides your development by logic—not luck. You'll discover how to make people enjoy accepting your ideas and wishes.

Principle #2 – Shows you how to get people to understand you, like you, believe in you, and trust you. You'll discover how to make a good impression which puts people on your side—anxious to help you.

Principle #3 – Shows you how to develop rapport with people who are important to your success. This step shows you the necessity of good communication.

Principle #4 – Shows you how to appeal to the "selfish" interests of people. You will learn how to motivate others to help you, by showing them how they can help themselves.

Principle #5 – Shows you how to want success more than anything in the world. Once you have convinced yourself that this burning desire must be fulfilled, your motivation for success will not be denied.

Principle #6 – Shows you how to use a balance of emotion and logic in winning others to your side, and making important decisions work.

As you apply the six principles of Human Engineering, you will not only discover a whole new way of influencing others, but you will also come to a better understanding of yourself.

DON M. GREEN
Executive Director
Napoleon Hill Foundation

How This Book Can Help You

How Important Is Your Future Earning Power?

If I asked you what the most important thing in life is to you, I believe your answer would be the same as mine. Next to your family and the spiritual things of life, it is your future earning power.

Now I didn't say your earning power. I said your *future* earning power. The past is prologue—only the future is yet to be.

This doesn't mean that in either your case or mine, our compulsion for service does not exceed our passion for gain. But actually it is through our financial ability that we can enjoy the good things of life, bring happiness to our loved ones and contribute our just share to civic and religious affairs.

Your Income is the Measure of Your Service to Others

We've all heard some people in the Business World throw off on money as though it were a wicked substance. They avow that their mission in life is not chasing the "Almighty Dollar."

I wonder if many of these people are not merely making excuses for their mediocrity. In reality, our financial income is the measure of our service to others. Money is just the method of keeping score.

Not too long ago my wife and I made the tragic mistake of forgetting to remove a baby tooth from under the pillow of one of our twin girls and to replace it with a quarter. As she tearfully came into our bedroom in the morning bemoaning her predicament I took her in my arms and pleadingly said, "Darling, you're a big girl now—you don't still believe in fairies, do you?"

Through her tears she sobbed, "No, Daddy, but I still believe in money."

I hope you believe in money because if you follow the principles outlined in this book, one of the normal and natural consequences will be that more money will flow your way.

Why are 20% of the People Responsible for 80% of the Results?

In pushing back the walls of understanding, in climbing the mountain to get a little fuller perspective of life, let's consider this very important question:

Why is it that in practically every field of endeavor we invariably find that 20 per cent of the people are responsible for 80 per cent of the results and that the remaining 80 per cent of the people are responsible for only 20 per cent of the results? Why is it that in a society of equal opportunity we have such unequal results?

NOT A NEW QUESTION

This is not a new question. For years, theories have been presented—concepts advanced, to explain why there is this great imbalance of results in a business world of balanced opportunity. Economy prognosticators and consultants in all fields are constantly offering new explanations. There is no subject in the entire spectrum of our business world today about which more has been written or spoken in the past than this particular question.

HUMAN ENGINEERING IS THE ANSWER

Finally, after much study and research over a long period of time, the definite consensus is that the answer lies in HUMAN

ENGINEERING. Yes, constant examination has verified and experience has certified this to be true. In fact, the years are punctuated with proof of this fact.

REASON FOR UNEQUAL RESULTS
BY THOSE WITH EQUAL OPPORTUNITY

The reason that the small 20 per cent, this successful few, are responsible for 80 per cent of the results is because this 20 per cent put 80 per cent importance on the human engineering principles and only 20 per cent importance on knowledge of their product or service.

Somewhat repetitious and redundant, but stated in another way, the reason the larger 80 per cent, the marginal producers, are responsible for only 20 per cent of the results, is that they put only 20 per cent importance on the human engineering principles and 80 per cent importance on knowledge of their product or service.

Yes, the answer lies in human engineering.

KNOWLEDGE IS NECESSARY BUT NOT ENOUGH

Before defining human engineering, let me make myself clear on one point from the very beginning. I am not throwing off on product knowledge. I am not discounting the importance of knowing and understanding the nature of our business, industry or profession. This is a necessity. Without it we are lost.

Furthermore, this knowledge must have its foundation in a constant learning process. School is never out for the "Pro." There is no saturation point. It is a constant journey and never a final destination.

I once heard a very astute man say, "A person who tries to succeed in any field of endeavor, without being knowledgeable in what he is doing, has just about as much chance of succeeding as a blind man, blind-folded, in a dark room, looking for a black cat that just isn't in there."

THE PLUS FACTOR IS HUMAN ENGINEERING—
KNOW YOUR PRODUCT BUT THINK PEOPLE

But knowledge of one's product or service, important as it is, is not enough alone, to put any individual into that fortunate 20% category. It's the PLUS factor added which makes the difference, and this PLUS factor is HUMAN ENGINEERING.

A man may be a walking encyclopedia of technical knowledge in his field. He may be the best informed person in his line of endeavor. But unless he has this PLUS factor to go along with it, he will remain in the mediocre category permanently. Yes, remember—know your product but think people.

WE ARE FIRST AND FOREMOST
IN THE PEOPLE BUSINESS

Human engineering is finally being accepted as the one most important factor in the entire pattern of economic success. First, foremost and above all else, we are in the people business. A person prepared "knowledge wise" and not conditioned "people wise" is just a failure walking around looking for a place to happen. Any knowledge of any kind to which we cannot apply the human equation and relate in some way to the problems of people, is about as useless as a sun dial in the shade. Fortified with only knowledge and not principles of human engineering, the person usually returns and says, "I received two orders—get out and stay out."

WHAT IS HUMAN ENGINEERING?

First of all, let's be sure we understand fully the meaning of HUMAN ENGINEERING. Perhaps in its simplest form, human engineering can be defined as the science of dealing with people— understand their responsive notes, their vulnerable spots, their "hot buttons."

An engineer is defined technically as one who is skilled in the art of planning, designing and managing in some particular field of endeavor. If a person concentrates his studies and activities in the field of managing people, he is engaged in human engineering.

Regardless of the business, industry or profession in which we are engaged, we are all involved to some extent in human engineering. Some of us naturally are more involved in human engineering than others, depending, of course, on the contacts we have with people. No one, however, is completely divorced from dealing in some fashion with other people. The day a person becomes more interested in people than abstract theories, he has taken a big step in the direction of becoming a human engineering expert.

LEARN THE THREE DIMENSIONS OF HUMAN ENGINEERING

Above all else, remember that the human engineer's concern is in three dimensions:

1. He does not stop with merely knowing WHAT people do.
2. He is not satisfied even with knowing WHY they do it.
3. He goes much farther. He also must know HOW to cause them to do it.

The human engineer is not satisfied with knowing only the behavior pattern of an individual, that is, knowing what he does.

He is not even satisfied with knowing the attitudes, tendencies or idiosyncrasies that cause him to do it.

The human engineer must go to the heart of an individual's existence and understand his ambitions, aspirations and goals in life—even his yardstick of values. He must understand these because he knows these are the qualities which cause the attitudes, tendencies and idiosyncrasies which eventually result in the behavior pattern of an individual.

THE ESSENCE OF SIMPLICITY

Our first impression might be that the human engineering approach is complicated—that it is composed of a lot of psychological "mumbo-jumbo." Actually, we can keep it simple and make it easily understood if we always think of these three dimensions in terms of the WHAT, the WHY and the HOW.

WHY ALL THREE DIMENSIONS

Years ago, human engineering was limited to a mere knowledge of behavior patterns. It was considered a great accomplishment to be able to predict WHAT a person would do under certain given circumstances. It was felt that if a person knew to some degree of accuracy what he could expect from an individual, he would have the advantage of not being taken by surprise. Thus, he felt some degree of security in planning his course of action.

It is true that there was a certain advantage in this. It was far better than being caught off-guard.

But this single dimension in understanding was far overrated.

THE SECOND DIMENSION

Then suddenly articles began to appear, books found their way into print, extolling the virtues of the second dimension—the WHY of human behavior. Many acclaimed this great innovation as a new day in the field of human engineering.

The word ATTITUDE became magic. It was the key to the second dimension—it became the great WHY word.

We were told that WHAT a person does, his behavior pattern, is nothing more than the result of his ATTITUDE. We were further assured that if we knew a person's ATTITUDE, at a certain time, we could predict with some certainty his behavior pattern so long as he maintained that same attitude.

It is true that this second dimension was another step toward the ultimate in human engineering. But it left much to be desired. Even with an understanding of this second dimension, we would have little assurance that a person's attitude would not change from time to time, with a resulting change of behavior patterns. Even if his attitude remained the same and if we had a fair knowledge of what would be his reactions, unless we had a deeper understanding of this individual, we could not influence his actions in any way.

THE THIRD DIMENSION

Although it might satisfy my curiosity to understand WHY a person acts in a certain way, unless I can do something to change his conduct to my liking, I do not receive the full benefits from human engineering.

For instance, I might know that a clock ticks. I might even know WHY it ticks. But unless I know HOW to wind it so that it will tick, I have accomplished nothing.

For instance, again, I may know that water boils at 100° Centigrade. I might be knowledgeable enough in my Physics to understand WHY it boils. But, again I say, that unless I know HOW to raise the temperature of water to 100° so that it will boil, I can accomplish nothing.

Translating this reasoning to the human equation, we may know that people act favorably when they are in a certain state of mind and emotion.

We may understand WHY this favorable action flows from such a condition of mind and emotion. But, still again, I say that unless we know HOW to create this condition of mind and emotion, we have very little control over the actions of others.

Yes, this third dimension of human engineering—the knowledge of HOW—introduced us for the first time into the creative world of action. With knowledge of HOW to cause people to act in a certain way, we have emerged from mere academic theory and climbed to a plateau of real accomplishment.

MOTIVATION, THE HOW WORD

Just as ATTITUDE was embraced years ago as the WHY word, MOTIVATION is accepted today as the HOW word.

People are moved to act only if they are motivated. I may inform, I may entertain, or I may educate a person, but until I have motivated him, he is not inclined to act as I desire.

This principle holds true so very strongly in the sales field. A person may know WHAT a prospect's buying habits are. He might even know WHY the prospect follows these buying habits. But the salesman will never be anything but an order taker, yes, an amateur, until he enters the great and magic world of creative selling by learning HOW to cause the prospect to change his attitudes and buying habits. He can only do this when he has learned the art of motivation. Yes, the HOW word, the third dimension, is MOTIVATION.

This principle is not confined to the sales field. It applies to every phase of our endeavors as long as we are dealing with people. And again I say that I know of no one on this earth who is not, to some extent, in the PEOPLE BUSINESS.

ACTION, ONLY EXCUSE FOR EFFORT

I cannot express too strongly the fact that in the field of human engineering, the WHAT and the WHY, are important to us primarily because they lead to the third dimension—the HOW.

The human engineer always looks for end results. He knows that any approach which does not bring forth end results is useless.

THE THIRD DIMENSION IN SIGHT—SOUND—
AND NOW HUMAN ENGINEERING

About the time of the turn of the century, three-dimensional vision was the rage. The stereopticon was the instrument of sophisticated home entertainment. What household would be without one?

A much shorter time ago, within the memory of most of us, we were introduced to three dimensional sound. Few homes can exist without the stereo.

Of far greater importance than either of these are the three dimensions of human engineering.

HUMAN ENGINEERING PERFORMS THE MIRACLE

Now that I have read my brief, I intend to present my case and demonstrate to you in what way human engineering is the PLUS factor which elevates a person from the marginal 80 per cent producer, to the fortunate 20 per cent.

This miraculous change from the Amateur Class to the Professional Status is contained in six magic principles of human engineering covered in the next six chapters.

The principles contained therein are not entirely new to you, I am sure. Most of us have heard them repeated over and over most of our lives. But unfortunately, few of us give them the importance they deserve and none of us use them to the extent they should be used.

Let This Miracle Happen to You

Now I hope you will study them carefully one at a time. Only after you have completely digested and assimilated a chapter, should you go to the next. Constantly refer back to each chapter until all six principles become a part of you—your subconscious as well as your conscious mind.

Don't even stop there. Begin immediately to use these great principles of human engineering. If you will do this and start immediately, you will find that miracles still happen and furthermore, that they can change your life almost overnight.

Now let's look to these six magic principles.

CHAPTER 1

(Principle #1)

PEOPLE LOVE TO BUY BUT THEY HATE TO BE SOLD

Sometimes we hear an important truth repeated so often that it loses the emphasis which it deserves. One such statement is this: PEOPLE LOVE TO BUY BUT THEY HATE TO BE SOLD. This is the first principle of human engineering. Mentally we know this, but actually only a few of us accept this in our dealings with others.

If I drove up proudly in a new car, would I say someone sold it to me? No, I bought it! I would be bursting with pride. Anything of which we are proud we acquired, we bought, we are the smart "cooky" responsible for our ownership. It is only those things of which we are ashamed that people sold us—yes, they were thrust upon us.

For instance, I once had a few shares of utility stock. These grew in price and in fact the stock was split once. Did anyone sell me this stock? No, I was smart—I was a Bull—I bought these pitiful few shares on my own judgment, uninfluenced by anyone.

But, unfortunately, I have enough uranium stock to paper my house. It's worth absolutely nothing. But did I buy it? No—some rascal of a salesman "high-pressured" me, against my will, and sold it to me. At least that's the way I feel about it now.

RELAXED RELATIONSHIP BETWEEN BUYER AND SELLER

How much more congenial would be the relationship between a seller and a buyer if the seller would take the attitude in his very approach that he is only assisting a person in doing what, under normal circumstances, he already wants to do, and, in fact, enjoys doing?

How much more relaxed would be the seller's entire demeanor? He would not be tempted to "high pressure" the buyer or be unduly aggressive in any way.

It is always a pleasure to assist a person in doing something which that person enjoys doing. There is no disagreeable aspect to the transaction and we, ourselves, are relaxed.

Since our own attitude is usually reflected in the attitude of the person with whom we are dealing, the purchaser also remains relaxed. We find that under these relaxed conditions, the relationship takes on the aspect of a "bridge" rather than a "wall."

DESIRE TO ACQUIRE AND OWN IS ONE
OF THE STRONGEST HUMAN IMPULSES

Does anyone doubt that people love to buy—love to acquire things?

The compulsion to acquire and own is one of the deepest of human impulses. It is not even restricted to the human race. Animals have a strong sense of possession. For instance, I have a dog that, under most circumstances, is a lazy and cowardly animal. Away from home he will run from another dog half his size. However, if another dog comes into his back yard, my old dog immediately is transformed into a ferocious beast that will go to any extent to protect his domain. He owns that back yard and he is proud of his possession.

The higher we go in the animal kingdom the more profound is the compulsion to acquire and own. Wars have been waged, vast migrations have taken place and new undeveloped countries have been settled in response to the compelling influence to acquire and own.

My wife would prefer to go shopping to acquire something than engage in any other activity. I only wish she had taken a course in college in *sales resistance*. If we happen to be stranded in a distant city for a few hours between planes, her favorite pastime is to go "window-shopping." What she can't afford to buy actually, she at least wants to buy mentally.

This desire to acquire asserts itself early in life. Babies cry for that which they see but can't reach. Small children fight over toys. As we grow older we continue to react to life's competitive system in an effort to get our share of the good things on this earth.

When as a youngster I got sick, my mother would give me a Sears Roebuck catalogue and a fifty cent piece and I would amuse myself for a full week looking through the catalogue and selecting, changing my mind, and selecting all over again, the article I wanted to buy.

Yes, the great desire to acquire, the compulsion to possess, is one of the deepest human impulses known to man. Since we can acquire in our modern economic system only by paying for things, we know full well that people love to buy.

WHY DO PEOPLE LOVE TO BUY?

But remember, we are human engineering experts. We are not satisfied just by knowing that people love to buy. We must move to the second dimension and know WHY people love to buy.

Psychologists have told us for years that the explanation is very simple. This great compulsion springs from the fact that it makes us feel important to acquire and own things, whether we need them or not.

We must keep up with the Joneses. We must show off that new car. We must move into that new house which is a status symbol.

Think back over the years to the first time you acquired some new possession. Do you remember that first bicycle, that first suit of long pants, that first party dress? Did you hide it or did you want to show it off? I'm sure, as I did, you wanted the whole world to know about it. And you saw to it that they did.

We don't even have to go back that far. Do you remember your first car, your first home? Can you recall recently the last thing of importance which you acquired? Didn't it give you a sense of importance to let others know about it?

How well I remember the first colored T.V. set we owned! It was the first in our neighborhood. The neighbors all came over to see it. It made me feel important. At first I only had it on a trial basis. But, after all, the neighbors had bragged about it, after my kids had invited all the kids within a mile to come and see it, it had taken on the role of a status symbol. Independent of the entertainment feature, it gave me such a feeling of importance that I couldn't have parted with it.

Yes, never forget that one of the prime reasons we buy things is that it makes us feel important.

THE MAXIMUM BUYING MOOD—HOW TO CREATE IT

But the fact that buying makes a person feel important is only part of the story. We have found in our research something far more important to us—something that is of vital importance to us in effective human engineering.

Not only does buying and acquiring make a person feel important, but consider this: *When a person begins to feel important and optimistic, he wants to buy and acquire.* He immediately enters his maximum buying mood.

Then doesn't it seem reasonable that if I want to sell you something, my first step should be to create this buying mood? And HOW is it done? It is very simple—by making you feel important and optimistic. This is the third dimension in human engineering. This is where we enter the creative world of *Motivation*. This is how we get action.

"Mr. Jones, I sincerely feel that you deserve this. You owe it to yourself after all these years."

"Mr. Smith, don't you feel that it's time that you start thinking of yourself a little bit?   You have everyone else on your payroll. Now honestly, isn't it time that you give yourself a little consideration?"

THIRD DIMENSION APPLIES TO EVERYONE

While many examples of principles contained in this book may be illustrated through the sales field, actually these principles apply just as strongly in every business, industry, or profession—in every walk of life.

We are all in the *People Business,* and because of this, no one is exempt from the necessity of being able to influence others. Civilization itself began when man first realized how far better it was to throw away his pre-historic club and resort to the method of influencing people to act as he desired. He has been refining this method over the centuries but, unfortunately, it is only recently that he has realized the full importance of the third dimension of human engineering—HOW to motivate a person to action by making him feel important.

"Mrs. Joy, it is only through the generosity of wonderful people such as you that this project is possible."

"Mrs. Johnston, if you will volunteer to assist in this community drive, your very example will influence others to do likewise."

"Mr. Boyd, we NEED people of your caliber to make this a success."

HOW TO MAKE ME FEEL IMPORTANT

As an example of creating the maximum buying mood, I relate a true incident which happened to me recently.

I walked into a store to look at some suits.   I had not really decided that I would buy one. As the clerk slipped a coat on me for size, I noticed the price tag on the sleeve.

Horrified, I said, "My friend, I don't want to buy the store—only a suit of clothes."

As I was grumbling and taking off the coat he said, "May I ask what profession you follow?"

"I speak at conventions and put on clinics and seminars throughout the country," was my reply.

He enthusiastically said, "Well, a person who does things that important, must *look* important. ISN'T THAT TRUE?"

Acting a little more interested I said, "I suppose so."

"That executive suit really makes you look important," he said admiringly.

The suit cost me twice what I had planned to pay for a suit. Also, it was a 42 short, and I wear a 44 long. But these had become minor considerations. The suit made me look IMPORTANT. This human engineer had motivated me. And how? By creating my maximum buying mood, he had made me feel IMPORTANT.

DON'T BLOW OUT MY CANDLE

Every person who approaches another in an effort to persuade him to act in a certain manner, should remember one fact above all else. If you are to be successful in the field of human engineering and motivation, you cannot afford to forget it.

You and I both, at all times, wear a big sign, "MAKE ME FEEL IMPORTANT—DON'T RAIN ON MY PARADE—PLEASE DON'T BLOW OUT MY CANDLE." If people in their mind's eye could see this sign on the other person and make full use of it by making him feel important before attempting to persuade him, these people would be far more successful in moving others to action.

Of course I am not referring to a sickening, nauseating massage of their ego. Nothing is more revolting or destroys a healthy relationship quicker then insincere compliments. The moment a person starts to give me insincere compliments, I begin to feel uneasy and want to get away from him as soon as possible.

BE SINCERE IN YOUR COMPLIMENTS

Many things can be camouflaged, but not *Insincerity*. This is a quality that is crystal clear at all times. People ARE important to

us and we should develop the habit of feeling that they are important to us.

If you doubt this, just try to imagine for a moment how you
would feel if suddenly you found yourself to be the only person on
this earth. It is almost horrible to think about. If you dwell on this
idea long enough, you will be amazed how attractive the next
person you see will appear to you.

I have a friend who makes his living by selling ideas to people
he has never seen before. He once told me that just before
approaching a prospect, he often imagines that he has just left a
desert island and this is the first person he has seen in a year. He
explained that this is the best insurance against treating his
prospect in a casual manner. This person suddenly becomes
fantastically attractive and important to my friend.

DON'T BE AFRAID TO COMPLIMENT

If you enter a person's office and see an ugly stuffed fish on the
wall, you can be sure, nevertheless, that this person is proud of it.
You can be certain that any favorable remark about that fish will
be received enthusiastically.

The same holds true with anything else which a person puts
on display. By merely putting it where it can be observed, he is
saying, "This is something of which I am very proud. Please let's
talk about it a few minutes before going into other matters. By my
very act of displaying it, I am bringing up the subject—this is one
of my favorite topics. Don't be rude and ignore my remark. If you
will take the time to chat with me for few minutes on a subject
which is important to me, you will find that I then have much
more time to talk about things that you consider important."

It is so very easy to find ways of making a person feel important. When we walk into a person's home for the first time, do we
have the habit of looking for something about which we can make
a favorable remark? Every home is a castle to someone—usually to
the owner.

Most people feel that they should be complimented on their

accomplishments and, in fact, feel neglected when these accomplishments go unrecognized. I am sure that if you picked, at random, ten of your friends and sent each one a telegram today and merely said, "Congratulations," you would find that eight out of the ten had, during the past week, done something for which they felt they should be congratulated.

GIVE THEM WHAT THEY WANT

Bernard Baruch is by all standards one of the greatest men of this century. He was an elder statesman, a financial genius, an adviser to presidents.

Just before he died someone asked him, "Mr. Baruch, if you could give one piece of advice on success, what would it be?"

Without a moment's hesitation he said, "Find out what people want, and give it to them."

People today crave, as they always have and perhaps always will, a feeling of importance.

Along with the sex urge and the law of self preservation, the compulsion to feel important has equal rank. From the time a person is born until he leaves this earth, he is engaged in a fanatical search for importance. First, he wants to be understood; then he wants to be accepted by his fellow man; finally, he wants his accomplishments to be recognized.

PEOPLE CRAVE IMPORTANCE

I have often read that three-fourths of the people on this earth go to bed every night hungry for food. All of us agree that this is a tragic situation. Personally, however, I feel that it is also tragic that nine-tenths of the people on this earth go to bed every night hungry for recognition—they crave to feel important.

None of us want to be thought of as a mere number, a digit, just a perforation on some punch card. In this technological age, don't think of me as a machine. Please don't forget that I am a person—don't thoughtlessly stick your finger in my eye and try to dial a number. Never lose sight of the fact that I am an individual, a human being—I have an unquenchable thirst for recognition, an appetite to feel important that is never fully satisfied.

If you and I, along with others, were part of a group picture, and if this picture were posted for observation, whose picture do you think I would look for? Do you think I would first be looking for yours? Don't kid yourself! I would be looking for my own.

YOU CAN BE A CREATOR OF CIRCUMSTANCES

When we have mastered this first great principle of human engineering, that people who have been made to feel important and optimistic enjoy accepting our ideas and buying our products, life itself will take on a new meaning. Then we can say that we are creators of circumstances, not creatures of circumstances; things will no longer happen to us, we shall happen to things; we shall then be the cause, not the result; people will be our opportunity, not our frustration; our fortunes will be guided by logic, not luck; our lives will be filled with magic, not mystery.

I urge you and I solemnly beg you to read, re-read and study this first great principle of human engineering. Constantly apply this principle until it becomes a part of you. The more you use it, the easier it will become and the more effective will be the results. Finally you will wonder how you were ever able to get along with people without using it.

CHAPTER 2

(Principle #2)

WE FIRST MUST SELL OURSELVES

Our second great principle of human engineering is certainly no less important than the first. Again I repeat that it is not new. But, unfortunately, too few of us stop and consider this principle before embarking upon the adventure of causing people to think and act in a predetermined fashion.

Before selling a person an idea or product, we first must sell ourselves. If a person doesn't like us, you can be sure of one thing—he doesn't like anything about our product or service.

It is one of the basic principles of human psychology that until a person first accepts us, he will not accept anything we offer. It is human nature to judge the dance by the dancer.

NO SECOND CHANCE AT A FIRST IMPRESSION

How often do you stop just before an interview and remind yourself that your prospect will not consider your product, service or idea until he has first formed an opinion of you. If his impression is not favorable, his mind snaps shut as tight as a steel trap.

This is why that first impression is so important. Some of our mistakes in dealing with people may be overlooked or even forgiven. But don't forget this cardinal principle of human engineering: *No one yet has been able to find a way to have a second chance at a first impression.*

We have been reminded over the years that a prospect's eyes are a camera and his memory a screen for the show. However, we forget too often that there is no "re-run." Furthermore, we are on stage only once—there is no opportunity for a rehearsal—no double feature. That first impression of us is all important. Is it any wonder that our first thirty seconds with a person are more important than thirty minutes thereafter?

WHAT WILL CAUSE HIM TO ACCEPT US?

Now, naturally, if a person will not accept anything we offer until he has accepted us, we ask ourselves, what are the qualities we must possess in order to have him like us and accept us?

From the beginning of recorded history, man has constantly sought to be popular—made an effort to have the approval of his fellow man.

In order to cause a person to accept our product, service or ideas, we must not necessarily win a popularity contest or be elected "Mr. Good Guy."   There are several basic qualities, however, which he must recognize in us if he is to accept us.

FIRST—BE YOURSELF

Please never lose sight of this important principle in dealing with people on a social, civic or business basis: *If you can't make a good impression being yourself, you certainly will "louse it up" trying to be something you are not.*

Most people are not only *likable* but even *lovable* when they can remember to be themselves. We only exaggerate our shortcomings and accentuate our faults when we try to be something which we are not. One of the greatest compliments we can pay anyone is to say how natural he is—nothing at all artificial or "put-on" about him.

How often have we heard the remark, "That person is so relaxing to be around, he is not at all exhausting. In fact, he is just like an old shoe."

It should not be difficult to *be ourselves,* but many people have acted in an artificial manner so long that they do find it very difficult. These people finally realize that they must take one step "outside" of themselves to arrive at their natural status.

So remember above all else, in our dealings with others, that if we want to be accepted, we must be natural.

SECOND—HAVE A HAPPY APPROACH

The sooner we realize that the world is a looking glass and gives back to every man a reflection of his own image, the nearer we are approaching that happy status of being a successful human engineer.

Never forget for even one moment that *everybody loves to be around an optimist.* The sweet magic of a cheerful disposition cannot be overrated.

DON'T tell people your troubles—DON'T be a crepe-hanger. People may be polite and appear to listen to our troubles, but they have troubles of their own. 80 percent couldn't care less and the other 20 percent are actually glad to find someone more miserable than they.

I could give you a sob story this very minute and I am sure you, too, could throw in the crying towel. For instance, I could tell you that I spend six days out of each week flying around the country at 30,000 feet above sea level, in an airplane made up of 15,000 parts, all put together by the low bidder. Practically every person I have ever met has more troubles than anyone else, and yet I have never found a person who has made himself more acceptable to others by advertising his troubles.

There is an excerpt from an anonymous prayer which should be remembered by us all, "Seal my lips from my aches and pains. They are increasing each day and love of rehearsing them grows sweeter as the years go by." As soon as a person learns that people as a whole are not concerned with his troubles, disenchanting as it may be, he will have made an important discovery of life.

REFLECT A HAPPY IMAGE

I have a dog named Sam. We don't know what kind of dog he is. We only know that he is a dog of very careless parentage.

Sam won't hunt, he won't point, he won't even catch mice. As a watchdog he is a disgrace. You could steal everything in my home and Sam couldn't care less. He would lick your shoes as you carried my possessions out and even help you if he could.

But in spite of his shortcomings, there is not enough money in existence to buy Sam from me. And I'll tell you why. When I come home at night my wife is often too busy to meet me. The kids are usually involved in their own interests. But not ole Sam! He will actually sit for five hours, if necessary, in front of the door waiting for me.

When I open the door, his old public relations department starts wagging. He makes me feel loved and wanted, but most of all, he reminds me of one of life's most important principles, which I repeat—that the world is a looking glass and gives back to every man a reflection of his own image.

I was speaking on this subject not long ago and a person in the audience said, "May I say something Mr. Robert?"

I said, "Of course."

He continued, "I am sure this principle works. I am a postman and now I understand for the first time why it is that I must look into the eyes of several people each morning to know how I feel."

TAKE TIME TO ENJOY PEOPLE

If we are too busy to enjoy people, they will not find time to accept us.

I once heard a person say, "In our mad, wild, fitful, feverish existence, many of us go through life like a man trying to read *Playboy Magazine* with his wife turning the pages."

No one enjoys the company of a man who seems too busy to converse with us in a relaxed manner. No one enjoys the company of a pessimist. If you want to place obstacles in front of you to make sure a person will neither accept you nor your ideas, just act as though you are a one-man grievance committee always in session. There may be some substitute for cheerfulness, but so far it has never been found.

Many people seem to be campaigning to be president of the Coronary Club or chairman of the Ulcer Derby.

THIRD—BE TRULY INTERESTED IN THE OTHER PERSON

Yes, in order to be certain that a person will like me and have confidence in me I must, first, be natural and, second, be happy and optimistic.

But these two qualities, alone, are not enough. If I want to be sure that I am accepted, by my very manner I must convince the other person that I am truly interested in him and all that concerns him.

TALK IN HIS FIELD OF INTEREST

I once heard a lady described as a remarkably well-informed person on a multitude of subjects. She was considered a good conversationalist. Her company was sought at any party or dinner she attended.

The fact was that this lady had learned early in life that if she directed the conversation into the field of the other person's interest, the conversation would always be spirited—it would never lag. I made a point of trying to find out her secret in this regard. Many times I heard her start out a conversation by asking her partner about something in the field of his interest. I have even heard her ask him what IS his field of interest. Then she started from there.

Anyone who talks only in the field of his own particular interest will find that only a few doors of conversation are open to him.

I have always been amused by the story of the "nouveau riche" millionaire who had made his millions from selling rat poison. He and his wife gave a big party on a certain occasion in an effort to enter the social world.

That night after all the guests had gone, the wife turned to him and said in an irritated way, "John, I did not see you engaged in conversation with a single guest all night."

In utter dejection he replied, "I tried a number of times but I couldn't find a single person who knew anything about rat poison."

SHOW THAT YOU ARE INTERESTED

I was privileged to speak at a medical convention not long ago. I arrived at the meeting a little early and I heard an elderly doctor giving advice to a group of young resident doctors. I was extremely interested in one statement he made.

> "Regardless of the medical knowledge you may have," said he emphatically, "you will never have a good practice or be considered a great doctor unless you have a compulsive INTEREST in your patients. Not only must you have this interest, but you must also be able to communicate to them clearly and convince them that you have this interest in them. Nature alone will cure most of your patients, unless you give them something to prevent their being cured. Furthermore, if during their period of convalescence, you are constantly interested in their welfare and they realize this, nothing will ever convince them that you alone were not responsible for their recovery."

Yes, never forget that before a person accepts any idea which we might present, he first must accept us—before he buys any product or service, he must first buy us. And furthermore, he will not accept us or buy us unless, first of all, we are natural in our approach; second, we are optimistic and have a happy approach; third, and finally, we are genuinely interested in the person we approach.

THIS PRINCIPLE VITAL TO THE SALES FIELD

I devote a large part of my time to sales clinics and seminars throughout the country. This second principle of human engineering is so vital to the salesman that I always try to impress him with the fact that if he neglects it, his entire interview is born dead.

The great Kettering painted the picture so beautifully when he said, "Before I buy a product or service, I first must buy the integrity, the enthusiasm, and the dedication of the person offering me that product or service."

A salesman, in particular, should form the habit of pausing just before an interview to remind himself that until his prospect has formed an opinion of him, he will not even consider the product or service. The prospect, in his thinking, finds it difficult to divorce the two.

A SALESMAN MUST SELL HIMSELF FOUR TIMES

But this initial sale of ourselves is not enough. A salesman must constantly resell himself throughout the presentation.

There are many formulae for a sales presentation. Practically all of them are good if they are used properly and constantly. None of them will work, however, unless WE do.

One of the most popular formulae is that contained in the following four steps: We must first secure ATTENTION, then INTEREST, next DESIRE and finally ACTION. For the sake of simplicity, many sales consultants speak of this method as the AIDA approach.

While this is an excellent approach, many sales organizations have failed to give this plan the depth approach it deserves, or to relate it to the human equation. I have been astounded to find that many large sales organizations merely teach their salesmen the "mumbo-jumbo" of the words without giving them the human engineering principles which apply to their use.

GIVE THE FORMULA—THE HUMAN EQUATION

Standing alone, the sales formula ATTENTION, INTEREST, DESIRE, and ACTION has very little meaning. But let's relate each of these to the human equation. Let's give each the THIRD DIMENSION approach, the HOW approach.

I first must be sure that a person UNDERSTANDS me so that I can get his ATTENTION. Next, I must cause him to LIKE me so that I can get his INTEREST. Then, I must be sure he will BELIEVE me so that I can convince him and create DESIRE. Finally, he must TRUST me so that he will ACT. Each of these constitutes a separate sale of myself.

And so the salesman who is determined to graduate into the 20 percent who are responsible for 80 percent of the results, must translate all he has learned into the third dimension. His first consideration must always be HOW to accomplish things. The WHAT and the WHY are important only to the extent that they help us understand HOW to proceed.

In many sales rooms where salesmen are trained, there are posted large signs which read:

1. I MUST FIRST GAIN *ATTENTION.*
2. I MUST THEN GET *INTEREST.*
3. I MUST NEXT CREATE *DESIRE.*
4. I MUST FINALLY GET *ACTION.*

I strongly recommended that we take a step forward and give a professional flavor to these signs—that we add the strength of the *Human Engineering* approach.

Why not change these signs to read:

1. HE MUST *UNDERSTAND* ME SO THAT I CAN GET HIS ATTENTION.

2. HE MUST *LIKE* ME SO THAT I CAN GET HIS INTEREST.
3. HE MUST *BELIEVE* ME SO THAT I CAN CREATE DESIRE.
4. HE MUST *TRUST* ME SO THAT I CAN GET ACTION.

THE PEOPLE APPROACH

The person who can translate these four elements of persuasion, namely ATTENTION, INTEREST, DESIRE, and ACTION, into the human equation will get results he never received before. Since we are in the PEOPLE BUSINESS we must make the PEOPLE APPROACH. This is the real HOW—the real third dimension.

For instance, it is not enough that I merely get a person's ATTENTION and INTEREST. This could either help me or hinder me in my goal. What I really want is his acceptable and favorable consideration.

If I am only interested in getting a person's attention and interest, I could walk through any business district and get all the attention and interest I desired. All I must do is walk into any establishment, kick open the president's door marked PRIVATE and say, "Hello, you big, fat, ugly baboon. I'm making a survey to see how 'touchy' people are. How is your blood-pressure, stupid?"

I am sure I can say with certainty that not only would I get ATTENTION and INTEREST but I would get ACTION as well. But what we really want is favorable ATTENTION and friendly INTEREST.

I do not subscribe to the philosophy of some people who believe that ATTENTION and INTEREST, as a last resort, should be acquired through the provocative approach—an approach that almost borders on an insult. This will not gain favorable attention and friendly interest and it is certainly not the *Human Engineering* and professional approach.

I believe I can go so far as to say that any sales organization that does not put full importance on the four great *Human Engineering* words, *Understand, Like, Believe,* and *Trust,* is not truly in the *People Business.*

BELIEF AND TRUST A NECESSITY

It took me years to understand fully and realize that a large percentage of the people who accept a product or service do so not because they are sure that it will solve their problem, but because they trust the individual, who offers it to them, and feel sure HE is convinced that it will solve their problem. Without the human engineering principles of BELIEF and TRUST, there can be no DESIRE and no ACTION. With them, we have professionalization at its best.

All six principles of *Human Engineering* are vital and important. But if I were forced to say that any one of them is more important than the others, I would select this second principle as set forth in this chapter. Carry this principle with you at all times. Concentrate on it before each interview.

DON'T FORGET THE FIRST BIG SALE

Again I emphasize the fact that, while many illustrations given in this book are taken from the sales field, the six principles of *Human Engineering* are equally applicable to every phase of our existence and in every walk of life. Regardless of whether you are a doctor, engineer, salesman, secretary or housewife, study this chapter over and over. Never forget that before any person will accept your ideas, products, or service, he first must accept you. That is why I stress so strongly that while you must know your product or service, still you must think people.

CHAPTER 3

(Principle #3)

PEOPLE ARE PERSUADED NOT BY WHAT WE SAY BUT BY WHAT THEY UNDERSTAND

"Isn't that what I said?"

"That is not what I told him."

"I was positive that I stated it as plainly as possible. How anyone could have misunderstood me is a mystery."

How often have you heard the above or some variation thereof?

If we went out and contacted a hundred successful business executives in any community and asked them what is the number one problem in the business field today, I am confident that 90 percent would say that it is lack of communication—lack of communication on a horizontal basis between employer and employee—short circuits in communication on a vertical basis between employer and employee—breakdown in companies and the public, distorting the image they are trying to build.

Competent research tells us that in 40 percent of the cases where an individual fails to persuade another, whether it be to buy a product, accept a service or work on a community project, the failure is not due to the fact that the person was not amenable to the idea, but rather due to the fact that he did not understand. A confused mind automatically says, "No."

I'LL GIVE YOU AN UNREAL OBJECTION

Furthermore, if a person does not understand, he does not like to admit it. If I confess that I am confused regarding some project or set of facts, I am afraid that in someone else's opinion I might appear stupid. It is so much easier to give you an unreal objection. I feel that I have accomplished the same purpose and still "kept face."

Much of this world's trouble is due to the fact that in our communications with others, we do not take the time to be sure that we are making ourselves clear. A complete and accurate understanding between two or more people is the best and, in fact, the only foundation for any successful relationship.

At an annual convention of the American Bar Association, a nationally known judge made the statement that over one-half of all the cases in the American courts today had their origin in some form of misunderstanding. He further stated that if people would take the time to be sure they were in perfect agreement before entering into a business transaction, we would need only about one-half of the courts we have today.

BREAKDOWN IN COMMUNICATION NOT RESTRICTED TO ANY PHASE OF LIFE.

This unnecessary "blind spot" in understanding is found in our everyday dealings, whether it be at work, at home or in our social affairs.

"I'm sorry! When you said 'Leave the valve open' I thought you meant the water valve."

"I don't see how you could have meant any other street corner except that one."

"When you said $18.00, I thought you meant a dozen for that amount."

"I don't recall that anyone ever told me that the meeting had been changed to Wednesday night."

All of us have had experiences in "short circuits" in communication.

I had one recently that I shall not soon forget.

Upon returning home late the other night I found a note on my pillow from my wife, "Regardless of what time you get in, call 266-3509."

I called the number and said, "Is this 266-3509?"

A rather sleepy voice said positively and in an irritated tone, "No, it is not!"

Rather confused I looked at the note again and said, "Are you sure this is not 266-3509?"

In a very pleading voice the person on the line said, "Friend, have I ever lied to you before?"

Somehow I felt the splinters of a fractured communication.

Near Douglas, Arizona, there is a fork in the road and each road has a sign which points to Fort Huachuca. I once heard a man say that he was confused by the two signs. He stopped his car at the fork, and seeing an old cowboy sitting on a wooden fence chewing a straw, said "Hey, Buddy, does it make any difference which road I take to Fort Huachuca?"

The cowboy, without changing his expression, lazily said, "Not to me, it don't."

Yes, I am sure that somewhere along the line there was a breakdown in communication.

Charley Clayton, an insurance executive in a very large Southern company, showed me a letter not too long ago which he had received from one of his employees with whom he was having some difficulty. As he handed me the letter he said, "Is it any wonder that we cannot communicate?"

I only read the first paragraph, "I know you believe you understand what you think I said, but I am not sure you realize that what you heard is not what I meant."

LET'S LOOK AT THE THIRD DIMENSION—THE HOW

But remember, we are not satisfied to know just the WHAT of any situation. We are not even satisfied to know the WHY. We are human engineering experts. Let's look to the third dimension of communication, the HOW. Let's consider HOW to avoid these pitfalls.

There is a simple formula for keeping open the channels of communication at all times. You will find that this HOW formula is being accepted everywhere today.

LET'S BE SIMPLE
LET'S BE RELATED
LET'S USE DRAMA

THE DIVINITY OF SIMPLICITY

Yes, first of all, unless we use the very essence of simplicity, we shall never get through to the other person.

Let's emphasize, let's repeat, let's ask questions, to be sure we are understood.

Let's explain carefully what we are going to say; let's say it; then let's repeat it; then let's tell them what we told them; finally let's ask sufficient questions to be sure there is no breakdown in communication.

QUESTIONS INSURE AGAINST MISUNDERSTANDING

Don't be afraid to ask questions. Questions are the greatest insurance policy against fractured communication. How often have you heard, "Why didn't you ask me?"

Did you ever hear, "If he had only asked me I would have explained it to him."

State often, "Am I making myself clear?"

Never use the question, "Do you understand?" If he doesn't, he will perhaps not admit it. Does he want to appear stupid? You bet your life he doesn't.

It has been said that a professional man is paid 60 percent for the questions he asks and 40 percent for the answers he gives. We are taught that in dealing with others it is more important to know the right questions than to know the right answers. The reason is that if we ask the right questions the right answers will be reduced to simplicity.

DON'T BE AFRAID YOU WILL INSULT WITH SIMPLICITY

It is true that we live in a more sophisticated society today than ever before. You might feel that because of the infinite care you take in presenting your ideas in a simple fashion, someone might feel that you are acting in a patronizing manner or even "talking down" to him.

We must remember that when we first approach a person on any idea, at the beginning he will give us only about ten or fifteen percent of his attention. Our explanation must be so elementary and direct that it will challenge even this small percent of attention.

Finally, as he begins to understand us, yes, and even begins to like us, he will become interested and consequently will give us a larger percent of his attention.

GREATNESS OF SIMPLICITY

Does it ever occur to us how many of the great enduring masterpieces of literature are the very essence of simplicity? Sometime, read the Lord's Prayer, the Twenty-Third Psalm, The Gettysburg Address, and the Constitution of the United States, looking primarily for the simplicity involved.

I personally feel that one of the greatest speeches, not only of this generation, but of this century, was that of Winston Churchill in which he momentarily awakened and solidified a nation. I defy anyone to mention any great speech with such utter simplicity of language. Just, for instance, consider these words, "Never in the annals of time have so many owed so much to so few." Was Winston Churchill afraid that he would insult his followers by using such simple language? I am sure he could have used big words if he had so desired because he was a master of the English language. Churchill knew that complete understanding and simplicity of expression go hand in hand and that one could not exist without the other.

COMPLEX AND INTRICATE VS. OBVIOUS AND SIMPLE

Too often we are looking for the complex and intricate and we fail to see the obvious and simple.

We remember the little school boy who wrote a note to his friend during a test, "Who the Dickens wrote the Tale of Two Cities?" The note was signed "Charles."

I heard someone say that if the safety pin had been invented today, it would have six moving parts, two transistors and need servicing twice a year.

There is a terrible coined word called *"Complexification."* Please never let its philosophy influence you in any way. It is dangerous. It may make an inexperienced speaker feel important, but it's the mortal enemy to good communication.

LET'S BE RELATED

Not only must we be simple and explicit in our dealings with others, but we must relate our explanations and stories to the understanding of the person to whom we are presenting our ideas.

For instance, do we approach a doctor, a lawyer, a farmer, a brick mason all in the same manner? Different words have different meanings to different people.

The word *"strike"* expresses the ultimate aim of a bowler. To a baseball player, it's a nightmare. To the head of a labor union it signifies one thing; to the manager of a large factory it undoubtedly stimulates a different emotion.

The word *"round"* has many, many different meanings. I am sure you can easily think of 5 or 6. I once read 16 different meanings.

Let us be sure that we mentally put ourselves in the shoes of the other person when we are presenting any idea of clarifying a situation.

I took one of my twins to an orthodontist. He took a good look at her teeth, turned to me, frowned and said, "She has a traumatic mal-occlusion."

He scared me almost to death. I thought I was going to lose her.

Why didn't he just say simply that she has a slight over-bite? I am no dentist—I couldn't understand the vernacular of the dental profession.

One of the first law suits I ever tried was in Lexington, Virginia. I was defending an insurance company in a suit arising out of an automobile accident. On direct examination, I asked a young doctor if his examination had revealed any injuries suffered by the plaintiff.

The young doctor elaborately examined the X-rays and his written report. He then turned to the jury and said slowly, "A careful examination reveals that there were no abrasions, adhesions, lacerations, fractures, or traumas of any nature as a result of the accident."

I then turned to the jury and said, "Before the doctor is cross-examined do any of you have any questions to ask?"

One member of the jury, dressed in overalls, turned to the doctor and said, "Doc, besides all those other things you said, can you tell me whether the guy was hurt in any way?"

Had the doctor been at a medical convention I am sure that there would have been complete harmony of understanding. However, he failed to communicate with the jury. He had not related his testimony to their understanding.

Recently, I witnessed a situation where there was complete communication because the person remembered to relate his presentation to the understanding of the listener.

I accompanied a real estate broker in a call on a cotton farmer to sell an income piece of property. The broker pointed to a couple of hundred bales of cotton and said, "Bill, just ten of those bales of cotton each year will make the payment on the mortgage."

This made so much more sense to the farmer than an intricate financial statement. I'm sure that if the purchaser had owned a dairy, the broker would have measured the mortgage payment in terms of milk from a certain number of cows.

Never lose sight of the fact that words have meaning only within the realm of the listener's understanding. If you would be a human engineering expert, your first consideration is the scope of your listener's experience and understanding—then you adjust your presentation accordingly.

LET'S USE DRAMA

Finally, in order to be sure that we are understood, not only must we be simple in our approach, not only must we relate our words and examples to the experience and understanding of the listener, but we must also be dramatic.

Shakespeare said, "The play is the thing."

It is certainly the best method of communication if we want to be sure that our message is understood. Throughout all history, the story has been the best vehicle to transport our ideas in an understandable and convincing way.

We learn in our study of literature that a drama is nothing more than a hero, a conflict and a happy ending. Of course there is the tragic drama also, but we are not here concerned with such.

Anytime we relate an example or a "for instance" we are, in reality, presenting a drama.

"Tom Jones, also, was undecided." Tom is the hero—his indecision is the conflict. "But he went along on this program and look at the successful results." The results constitute the happy ending.

EVERYONE LOVES STORIES

From the time we were tiny kids, we wanted to hear stories. All through the ages kids from five to ninety have been thrilled by dramatic recital of the hero, the conflict and finally the prince coming in on a white horse and saving the beautiful princess.

What is the most fascinating and understandable part of the

Bible? I am sure that many will tell you it is the parables—yes, the story of the Prodigal Son, the Good Samaritan and other recitals which carry a spiritual message forcefully presented through the three parts of the drama.

FEEL, FELT, FOUND

Psychologists and research centers for a number of years have been advocates of the Feel, Felt, Found method of presenting a drama. It is simple and yet most effective.

Let's imagine that I am presenting an idea to Mr. Jones or making an effort to sell him a service or a product. I am doing fine. I have complete empathy and harmony with him. As I raise my eyebrows, his automatically are raised; I scratch my ear and his begins to itch. I am positive that he will buy my idea completely and act in a manner predetermined by me.

Then suddenly something happens. He "freezes." I have lost him completely.

Many people worry about "post decision remorse." My concern here is "predecision paralysis."

What do I do? Do I "move-in" and try to get a quick decision in order to save the situation? That is exactly what I should do—if I want to lose completely.

No, I resort to the fabulous Feel-Felt-Found formula, which, if used correctly, can be magic.

I relax, hoping that by my example Mr. Jones also will relax.

"Mr. Jones, I know exactly how you feel."

Now he knows that I am in his corner—not across the ring from him as his opponent. He feels understood, which is important.

"In fact, Mr. Jones, many have felt just as you do."

Now, Mr. Jones relaxes even further. He is sure that his doubts are not serious—others have had them also—he is not alone in his fears.

"But this is what they have found, Mr. Jones."

Since 95 percent of the people are followers and only 5 percent are not, Mr. Jones is inclined to go along with the majority—yes, with those who overcame the conflict, had a happy ending and became heroes.

ENJOY THE MAGIC OF STORIES

I repeat that the drama is the greatest vehicle which has been discovered to carry ideas into understandable and acceptable areas of a person's thinking. The drama has been used for this purpose for thousands of years. Sometimes, however, we forget its effectiveness. Don't you fail to use it on every occasion possible. The story form of presentation is the very best possible insurance against any chance of misunderstanding.

And so, as we end this chapter, I urge you strongly to concentrate on the three methods contained herein when next you are engaged in persuading a person to accept your ideas or follow a certain line of conduct.

First of all, be sure your approach is the essence of simplicity and furthermore that your entire presentation remains elementary and understandable throughout.

Next, mentally put yourself in the shoes of the person to whom you are speaking. The words you use, the examples you give and the "for instances" you present, must all be in the realm of his experience and his understanding.

Finally, generously use stories in illustrating your points. The drama cannot be surpassed or even matched in its power to communicate and persuade. Everyone loves a hero. We unconsciously identify ourselves with him. The effectiveness of the drama is fabulous in results if we will only remember to use it. Don't you pass up this great opportunity.

CHAPTER 4

(Principle #4)

HOW DOES IT BENEFIT ME— NOT YOU, BUT ME?

One great lesson in human engineering often brings disenchantment with it. And yet, it is a lesson we all must eventually learn.

Our ideas, products or services are acceptable to an individual only to the extent that he feels they will benefit HIM. Nothing we can offer anyone has any value within itself if divorced from the human equation. This is why the human engineer never mentions features unless he follows up his remarks by translating the features into benefits.

"This model has the automatic changer, which means, Mr. Smith, that a great deal of time is saved."

Chances are that Mr. Smith doesn't know what an automatic changer is, nor does he care. He is, however, interested in saving his valuable time.

It is only the rank amateur, the inexperienced person in the "people business," who is a "feature yakker." He elaborates on the physical qualities of a product and completely ignores the human equation.

Pick up a national publication and thumb through it, studying the advertising. Do the large milk companies any longer sell milk, telling of its qualities?   No, they sell healthy babies—only the advantages of their product.

Do you read any longer of some major automobile company advertising some convenient type of gear shift?   No, but we read of a "rush of power in a hush of luxury."

PLACE, TIME AND CIRCUMSTANCES

If our timing is off, value is immediately lost.
"How I wish you had spoken to me sooner about this."
"Where were you last week?"
"We can use your services next month but not at present."

Just as Einstein's Theory of Relativity added a fourth dimension, TIME, to the three other dimensions of space—length, width, and height—human engineering has added TIME as a most important factor in evaluating the benefits of any product or service.

Place and circumstances, also, are just as important when considering benefits and values.

If we lose sight of the time, place and circumstances of any product or service we will have lost sight of important elements in human persuasion.   For instance, if a man were dying from thirst in the middle of the Sahara Desert, would diamonds or gold or silver be of any value to him? I'm afraid he would not be interested. The possibility of securing one small cup of water would, I assure you, motivate him to a greater extent. This is an extreme case, but it illustrates a point that we too often overlook.

All of us know that a brand new Cadillac has value at times. But if you and I were drowning in the middle of a lake would this new Cadillac to keep up with the Joneses be of any interest to us? I am sure it would not. However, we would be very good prospects for a row boat.   We would not even "dicker" on price.

Since a person is primarily interested in the needs and benefits to HIM of anything we offer and since benefits are determined primarily by time, place and circumstances, we must view the entire situation before making an approach.   Something might be extremely valuable to us at one time and under certain circumstances and yet absolutely worthless to us on some other occasions.

Then can't we see how important it is for us to consider first the individual and all elements of his situation before even thinking of the ideas, products and services we might intend to offer? This is the very basis of human engineering.

NOT YOUR PRODUCT OR SERVICES BUT MY NEEDS

We hear much these days about the importance of believing in an idea, product or service. It is certainly true that before we can get anyone else to accept an idea, we first must have accepted it ourselves. We cannot sell an idea until we ourselves have bought it, any more than we can come back from some place we have never been. Yes, we cannot give that which we do not have.

And yet, important as this principle is, it has a hidden danger. Because I believe so strongly in the idea or product that I shall present to you, often I ignore your problem or needs in my enthusiasm for that which I am to offer.

DON'T TALK TO YOURSELF

Please always remember this. Until you and the person you approach have first agreed completely upon what his problem is, you are not talking to anyone except yourself. Think about this. You may be able to make a brilliant presentation on the unsurpassed qualities of a certain service or product but until you first have fixed a need in someone's mind, your brilliance falls upon deaf ears. You're only pounding your own ear drums.

The next time you approach a person in an effort to get him to accept some project or service, try this method. Forget about what you have to offer at first. Concentrate on HIS needs, HIS problems. Not only is this the proper sequence of a presentation but you will find that in the beginning he is far more interested and will warm up much quicker if the conversation is limited in scope to the field of things that concern him.

If you and I can first agree that I have a real problem and furthermore if we can pinpoint and fix this problem with exactness, be assured that I shall be looking for the solution with much more concern than anyone else.   Then, at this time, if you offer me ideas, services, or a product that will bring about the solution to this problem, I shall be just as enthusiastic to accept what you present as you will be eager to make the offer.

LET'S FIRST TALK ABOUT ME

I am an easy person with whom to get along.   I dislike ever offending anyone.   If I should accidentally hurt your feelings, I would be miserable; believe me, I would.

But, please remember this.   If you come to me with a product to present, I couldn't care less about that picture of your new factory.   It's of little concern to me that you operate in fifty states. The history of your great founder, interesting as it may be to you, leaves me cold.

All I want to know is: Can you help me solve my problem?

WHAT WILL THE PRODUCT DO FOR ME?

And there is one thing certain.   You cannot solve my problem or bring me benefits until first you discover, with my help, what my problem is.

So, let's first talk about me—my favorite subject—not you, your company, your service or your product.   Begin asking me questions, show a genuine interest in me. If you do, I am sure to listen. If you don't, I don't hear a thing you say.

GET ME TO AGREE WITH YOU WHAT MY PROBLEM IS

Until I have agreed with you on my specific problem, you cannot solve this problem any more than you can paint a picture on a canvas which is not there or carve a statue from stone that does not exist.   One of the frailties of human nature is that people lose sight of the orderly sequence of human events. To offer any advantage or benefit before establishing its need or benefit is truly trying to create a rope out of sand. Whatever else you do, don't make this mistake.

PLEASE ASK ME QUESTIONS

You may be selling the finest skis on the market. If you offer me these at 40 percent off, I assure you I am not interested. If you offer them to me at 60 percent off, still I am not interested. You might even offer to give them to me—I'm still unmoved.

WHY? Because if you had taken the time to ask me questions, you would have found that while I may have some hobbies, skiing is not one of them.

Maybe you have heard of the little old lady who went into a gas appliance store to buy a heater. The eager salesman, more enthusiastic than experienced, launched forth into an ecstatic dissertation over the merits of a certain heater on display. He explained in great detail the B.T.U. factor, the air displacement in terms which he claimed made it an engineering miracle.

Finally, after he became exhausted, he momentarily stopped for breath. The little lady, with a blank expression on her face, said gently, "All I want to know is, will it keep a little old lady warm?"

A human engineer never becomes so interested in means, methods, and tools that he forgets end results.

DON'T FORGET MY PROBLEMS MAY CHANGE

Even if you are engaged in a business which is serving me at present and solving my problems, don't forget that my problems may change or even increase. If this should happen, I shall expect you to offer new solutions and keep pace with changing conditions. Keep in touch with my problems. You, perhaps, through your knowledge and experience, will find it easier to recognize these changes than I do.

Please don't feel that I should be loyal to you and continue to use your services any loner than you merit my loyalty. You will merit this loyalty in the future only as long as you offer me new benefits to solve my changing or increasing needs.

WHAT HAPPENED TO THE OLD OAKEN BUCKET?

Did it ever occur to us to wonder what might have happened to the "old oaken bucket?" It was the hallmark of an era. Songs were written about it. It was symbolic of gracious living.

But the romance of the oaken bucket was short lived. It had no permanent franchise on existence. The galvanized tin bucket replaced it. Although the tin bucket did not look as glamorous, it was lighter and cheaper.

But even the tin bucket had no hold on permanence. It has now been replaced. The plastic bucket costs less and is still lighter.

Did sentiment on anyone's part of loyalty to the bucket companies make any difference? For a certainty, it did not.

The bucket companies went out of business because they forgot something. They thought that they were selling buckets, when in reality they were selling containers of water. They lost sight of the problem they were supposed to be solving.

This is significant in all facets of our economy.

Wouldn't you have thought that the railroads would have been the owners of our air lines today. Not one of them is such an owner. And why? Because they too forgot something. They thought they were in the business of railroading, when, in fact, they were engaged in transportation. They forgot to keep pace with changing times. They left it to someone else to offer a quicker form of transportation.

Again, wouldn't you have thought that the great moving picture companies would have become the owners of our broadcasting facilities? They didn't. Again, why? Because they considered themselves as being in the picture business, when in truth they were in the entertainment business.

YOU CONCENTRATE ON THE PROBLEM

Please don't underestimate the importance of this fourth great principle of human engineering. Nothing that is offered has any value within itself if divorced from someone's needs. Only to the extent that it solves someone's problem has it any value at all. As human engineers, let's first concentrate on the individual—his needs—his problems. Then the door is open to present our ideas, our product or our service.

CHAPTER 5

(Principle #5)

WANTS, NOT NEEDS, CAUSE PEOPLE TO ACT

Even if we are problem minded and have discovered the need of the other person, this means nothing until we can cause him to WANT what he NEEDS. This is perhaps the hardest principle of human engineering for the average person to accept.

"Yes, but he NEEDS this—yes, he needs it above all else."

This doesn't mean a thing unless he also wants it.

Needs move a person only when he is in a state of desperation. Wants are a magic ingredient. They are emotional, sentimental; they have no ceiling, no limitation. Wants alone bring out the best within us.

If wants did not have a greater moving power than needs, then tell me why there are so many more television sets in this world than there are bath tubs.

WE ARE A "WANT PEOPLE," NOT A NEEDY PEOPLE

We are not, and probably never will be a needy people. If we want certain things in life badly enough, we automatically draw upon those resources within us and convert them to productivity. We might have needed certain things for a long time, but until we finally begin to want them, we shall certainly never get them, unless by accident.

Many people who merely need things sit idly by and dream of the joys they will experience when their dream ship comes in. We all realize that this is the only sure way of "missing the boat." But the man who really and truly wants something, knows that the ship of opportunity is already docked for him, and is only waiting for him to unload its priceless cargo.

GIFT OF DISSATISFACTION AND DIVINE DISCONTENT

To meet with any measure of success in this life, we must have the gift of dissatisfaction. We must want circumstances to be better than they now are. If we are completely satisfied with our present state of life, and with everything that surrounds us, the pilgrimage has ended for us and we have already settled in our little city of compromise. We are then bogged down in the quicksands of complacency, lost in the sterile valley of inertia, and frozen in the ices of status quo. It is only through divine discontent that we keep moving forward.

GRATIFICATION OF WANTS—
NOT SATISFACTION OF NEEDS

No little girl actually needs a ribbon in her hair. My kids don't need a colored television set, or any television set, for that matter. But what would happen to the ribbon factories—what would happen to the thousands of T.V. jobs if we restricted ourselves only to satisfying needs?

The greatest economy in the world—the highest standard of living on the face of this earth—has been built on the gratification of WANTS, not the satisfaction of NEEDS. This is responsible for the fact that we live in a country, with only 7 percent of the world's population, living on 6 percent of the earth's soil and yet we enjoy 53 percent of all the world's luxuries.

I heard a prominent business analyst make the statement, with which most merchandise research centers agree, that if the public began buying only what they needed, the entire economic system of America would begin disintegrating within 120 days.

IMMEDIATE IMPULSE VS. ULTIMATE PURPOSE

Making a person want what he needs, more than he wants what may gratify a temporary desire is often not easy.

Maybe I need more insurance for my family's protection, but can you make me want it more than I want a trip to Honolulu?

Maybe I need a sound savings plan to give me ultimate security, but do you know how to make me want this more than I want to join a new gun club?

Causing a person to want what he needs, more than he wants what he doesn't need, is a great challenge to the human engineering expert. It's a real character sale. Remember, there is always the great temptation for a person to gratify his immediate impulse rather than accomplish his ultimate purpose. It is so much easier. Our challenge is to see that he doesn't yield to this temptation.

FIRST FIND HIS DOMINANT DESIRE

It is elementary that before we dive into water, we first test its temperature and depth.

Also, before attempting to cause a person to act in a predetermined manner, it is important to find his responsive note, his vulnerable spot or his "hot button." Everyone, unless he is a complete vegetable, will respond to a least *one* of the five motivating factors: *Pride, Profit, Need, Love,* or *Fear.*

Our responsibility is to find, by testing, just which one of these factors motivates an individual most strongly. If we proceed systematically, in an orderly manner—not haphazardly—and carefully study the individual thoroughly, we are bound to find the responsive note in one of these five motivating factors. We might sometimes be required to run the entire gamut of all five factors, but the response is there and if we proceed properly we shall find it.

CONCENTRATE ON JUST ONE MOTIVATING FACTOR

Now this is important. When you have found the one responsive note, you should skip the other motivating factors and concentrate on this one alone. Most people are moved to action by one persuasive point. If we try to cover all the other points, after we have found the one dominant note, we shall only bring about confusion and we shall destroy the effectiveness of our efforts up to this point.

If you are sure you have determined which is the prime motivating factor to which an individual responds, forget all the others and concentrate on that one point. This is the only sure method of making a person WANT what he NEEDS.

If, however, we do not look for this one responsive note, but merely proceed in a "catch as catch can" fashion, we shall find that we are not conducting ourselves as human engineering experts. We shall not motivate people to the desired action.

Regardless of what business, industry or profession you are engaged in and regardless of what line of endeavor you pursue, you will be more effective in influencing others if you carefully organize your approach and direct it to only one point of interest.

Let's consider a few examples of these five motivating factors. I am sure you can formulate examples that will apply to your particular endeavors in life, whatever they might be. They are equally important and applicable whether you are persuading your children or some other loved one to act in a certain manner or whether you are trying to sell pots and pans to a housewife or airplanes to a large company.

To illustrate these five motivating factors, I shall assume that I am attempting to interest an individual in purchasing a home. As I present some advantage directed to each of these factors, I am holding my prospect's mental pulse, watching him carefully to detect any response. As soon as I get the response, I ignore the remaining motivating factors and concentrate on the one responsive note.

PRIDE

"Mr. and Mrs. Jones, as you can appreciate, there are few homes in this entire city which have the beauty, the artistic construction, the tasteful landscaping and many other desirable features which this home has. It's a home that both you and your children can be proud of and will take pride in owning as long as you live."

Be careful to note that the features are quickly translated into the human equation, the benefits that they will enjoy. They will be *Proud* and take *Pride* in their ownership.

PROFIT

Maybe the couple responds very little to *Pride*. Perhaps they are very frugal people and put emphasis on the monetary consideration.

"Mr. and Mrs. Jones, this fine house, as you can readily see, is well constructed and will endure through the years with a minimum of maintenance. It is also designed with many outstanding architectural features that will not become outdated or obsolete in the future. It is also situated in a fine residential area where values have constantly been going up. These features are worth money to you, because if you ever have to move and sell this property, it will show very little depreciation. In fact, you might be able to sell it for a profit."

NEED

If profit is not the vulnerable spot, I show no signs of discouragement. Enthusiastically I go to my next motivating factor: Need.

This is the most basic of all motivations. I know there is a definite need for my product or I wouldn't be engaged in the business of offering it. Yes, I repeat, my job is to make my prospect want what he needs. Until I can make him want it and make him want it more than he wants the money it takes to buy it, I cannot reach his vulnerable spot.

"Mr. and Mrs. Jones, this beautiful home is exactly the right size for you and your children. In fact, from what you told me, if you had designed a home for your particular needs, this would be it. The play room is far enough removed from your study, Mr. Jones, that there will be no disturbing noise."

LOVE

If I still don't get a response, I am not discouraged. *Love* is a powerful motivating factor. I stay enthusiastic at all times.

"Mr. and Mrs. Jones, you can see how well this beautiful home adapts itself to you and your children. With the big living room and family room the home is deserving of a family that is close and who enjoys being together."

FEAR

Fear of loss moves people to action perhaps quicker than any other factor—certainly much quicker than desire for gain.

"Mr. and Mrs. Jones, the rolling surge of inflation is robbing the dollar, which we work so hard to save, of its value. The purchase of real estate in a growing area is about the best and, in fact, about the only hedge against inflation. This is a good investment—one you can't afford to miss."

Don't overlook the power of fear of loss. A leading industrialist once said, "I wouldn't keep my business open all night to make $100, but I would stay up all of seven nights to keep from losing $100."

I am in a little syndicate with six people in Arizona. On five occasions we have put into the pot a certain amount of money to drill for oil in northern Arizona. It always turns out to be a dry hole. Now, I have just been notified by our chairman that they are ready to go again. I know we won't hit oil. Then why am I putting in my share? Because if they hit oil and I were not in the syndicate, I'd die! Yes, the fear of loss is going to keep me in there as long as they drill and as long as I can continue to borrow money to put in my share.

I HAVE A RESPONSIBILITY

If I am engaged in selling a service or product to an individual and if it is determined that the individual needs my service or product, then I have a responsibility to make that individual want it. The best method for me to use in carrying out my obligation is to be knowledgeable in the use of these five motivating factors.

Also, it will help us to carry out this obligation if we never lose sight of this principle: A person pays for what he needs, whether he buys it from us or not. Think about that. I repeat, a person pays for what he needs whether he buys it from us or not.

Sometimes he pays for it in coin of the realm and sometimes he pays for it in more expensive currency—such as causing himself and his family to sacrifice pleasures to which they are entitled.

As an example: "Mr. Jones, do you realize you could own this beautiful home for payments less then those you are now paying for rent?"

"Mr. Smith, do you realize that repair bills are costing you more on your old car than payments would amount to on a new car?"

"Mr. Pleasant, the gamble you are taking on your boy's education is too grave a risk compared to the small payments on this educational policy."

If I am already paying for something in money, sacrifice, or risk, I feel I am entitled to it—yes I *want* it.

This fear of not receiving something for which we are already paying moves a person to *WANT* it in practically every instance.

TAILOR MADE FOR ME

Just one approach in causing a person to *want* what he needs, is based on the following principle:

"A bargain is measured, not in terms of dollars and cents, but rather by how nearly something comes to solving my problem." Here we have to assume completely the role of a *"problem solver."*

A ten room home out in the desert at half price is no bargain for a widow who lives alone and wants to be near her church, doctor, and a shopping center. At a price even half of that, it's no bargain. Why? Because it doesn't solve her problem and she doesn't want it.

A studio apartment might be a great bargain for an artist, but to a doctor who wants his office in his home, it might be completely unacceptable.

Show me something which is tailor made to my needs and I begin wanting it. We pay more for a tailor made suit, a custom made house, because we WANT it enough to be willing to pay more.

Let me feel something is practically made for me, and I'll want it.

"That dress, Mrs. Jones, looks as though it were actually designed for you."

"Mr. Smith, they must have had you in mind when they made that coat."

BE A WANT CREATOR

Don't neglect this fifth great human engineering principle. Before people will buy, they must be encouraged to WANT what they NEED—yes WANT it more than something else—yes, even more than they want the money it takes to buy it.

CHAPTER 6

(Principle #6)

EMOTION OPENS THE DOOR BUT LOGIC LOCKS IT TIGHTLY

Practically all who study the field of persuasion agree that approximately 85 percent of the decisions in life are made by a person while he is in an emotional frame of mind and that only approximately 15 percent are made purely on logic. This does not mean that logic is of only 15 percent importance in considering decisions, as we shall see later.

Someone once described an indecisive person as "a confused conglomerate of molecules headed in a not too well defined direction, looking for a catalytic agent to precipitate him into a decision." We all know that emotion is the strongest catalyst that exists.

BUT EMOTION ALONE IS NOT ENOUGH

All of our lives we have been taught that decision making is primarily heart appeal rather than mind appeal—emotionalization rather than rationalization.

But emotion, important as it is, is not enough alone to insure that a decision will be permanent. Emotion is a transitory thing— it comes and goes. Then doesn't it seem understandable that if a decision is supported by emotion alone, as soon as the emotion subsides, there is nothing to support the decision and hold it up. It comes "unglued."

POST DECISION REMORSE

People who make decisions while in an emotional state of mind, and whose decisions are based on pure emotion, usually develop "post decision remorse." How many times have you heard the following:

"I don't know, for the life of me, what caused me to do that."

"Could I have been in my right mind?"

"I don't know why I let him talk me into it. It seemed a good idea at the time."

Have you ever bought something in a time of excitement and later tried to understand how you ever possibly could have bought it? Your decision was made in a climate of emotion, but your self analysis was later made in the atmosphere of logic.

GIVE IT THE TEST OF COLD LOGIC

Did you ever hear a person say, "Well, I want to sleep on it?"

What he is really saying is that he wants to wait until after the glow of emotional enthusiasm has subsided and examine the situation in the cold light of reason and logic.

I once heard an old homespun philosopher say, "I don't like to make up my mind all at once. If it sounds as good tomorrow as it does today, I'll go along with it."

Here again was a situation where a person wanted to be sure that his decision would be given the blessing of logic.

PUT IN THE RIVETS OF LOGIC

Even if a person makes a decision based purely on emotion, one can drive in the rivets of logic to cause the decision to remain "fixed."

Let's imagine that a man bought a home and that he was influenced to buy primarily because of the pride of ownership and the luxury and comfort which he felt it would bring him. Later he analyzes the situation and the fear begins to haunt him as to whether he should spend so much money for such luxury and comfort. Maybe he experiences "post sale remorse." He regrets his decision and wonders if he can change his mind.

If, however, at the time he decided to buy the home, someone had approached him in this manner, "I know you are happy over this purchase. I am sure that you and your family will enjoy all the many conveniences and luxuries which this home will bring. But don't overlook the fact that this is a good business transaction also. I feel confident that prices will continue to go up in this area. You can have no better guard against inflation. You may find times when the payments require some planning but your accumulated equity will act as a secure savings plan. In fact, Mr. Jones, I congratulate you on a good business investment."

GIVE HIM A GOOD REASON FOR
DOING WHAT HE WANTS TO DO

Now what has been done? He has been given a logical reason and an excuse for buying what he wanted to buy. He now feels justified in doing what he did. Even though the emotion might subside, as it is bound to do sooner or later, because emotion is transitory, the logical reason is still there.

Did you ever have some friends tell you of a trip they were about to take and have them urge you to join them? Maybe you became excited over the idea of doing some enjoyable things and at the moment you decided it was an excellent idea. The next day or maybe even that night, when the excitement had subsided, you changed your mind.

But what if your doctor had told you the same day that it was imperative for you to take a vacation? He told you that unless you immediately took some time off from your work, you would be flirting with disaster. Now the situation is entirely different. You have been given a logical excuse for taking the trip that you wanted to take in the first place. It would be a calculated risk to your health if you didn't take the trip. Strong rivets of logic have been added to the original emotional decision. The decision does not come apart.

BALANCE OF LOGIC AND EMOTION

Very few people ever realize that in the field of human engineering, every day we weigh logic and emotion against each other in making the decisions.

For instance, you see in a store window a good looking suit that catches your eye. You are immediately motivated to go in and see if your size is in stock. You feel excited and emotional over the idea.

Then logic takes over and works against your decision to buy. You have just noticed the price. It is far beyond what you feel justified in paying for a suit.

Emotion moves back into the picture. This is the suit that you have been waiting for. It is not just an ordinary suit. You once saw a person wearing such a suit and you resolved that some day you would have such a suit if you could find one.

You now begin looking for a logical excuse to do the thing you emotionally desire to do.

After all, this is the suit you have been trying to find. Maybe you will not find it again. Don't you feel obligated from a business point of view to look nice? This is really a business investment as much as anything else. It is not as though you planned to wear this suit only on social occasions.

Now, what are you going to do? You are weighing the logical reasons against the emotional reasons. You want to feel justified in buying the suit, but on the other hand, you don't want to let your emotions run away with you. You are looking for that excuse to do what you really want to do.

PLEASE GIVE ME AN EXCUSE

I have a friend in the autumn years of his life who takes two drinks each night before dinner. He confided in me that for a long time, he really didn't fully enjoy this because his conscience hurt him. He was not sure that he was justified in doing this.

Finally, his doctor told him that this was a very fine thing to do for his health, provided that he limited himself to two drinks. In fact the doctor said he would perhaps live a longer and more relaxed life if he never forgot to take the drinks.

Now my friend revels in the activity. He makes quite a ceremony out of his two drinks. He has not told me once but at least a dozen times as he smiles and sips his drinks that he is only conscientiously following doctor's orders.

I recently met a very wonderful elderly man on a vacation in Honolulu. He was really "living it up" to the extent his years would permit. In fact he was the life of the party and his enthusiasm was contagious. When I first met him, he elaborated on the fact that he was taking the vacation in Honolulu only because his doctor had insisted he needed the trip. He said that his doctor left him no choice in the matter. Then with tongue in cheek he smiled and with a twinkle in his eye said, "Also, my friend, at my age, every day has got to be a winner."

I'll never know who this man's doctor was and in fact I don't even remember the man's name, but somehow I am confident in my own mind that he was a great doctor, a doctor not only with medical knowledge, but a doctor who was a real human engineer also.

EMOTION TEMPERED WITH LOGIC

Because I have stressed the fact that emotion standing alone is often hazardous, please don't lose sight of its significance. However, it is important that we temper it with a reasonable amount of logic so that it will have permanence to it. Logic gives to emotion the same strength that carbon gives to steel.

It is important that we are able to appraise this balance between emotion and logic, whether we are attempting to sell an idea, product or service or we are considering the acceptance of such. The proper proportion of these two important ingredients determines the stability of our very existence. Consider them carefully. Learn to evaluate them. They are the two important tools used by one who has mastered this sixth great human engineering principle.

START USING THESE PRINCIPLES TODAY

These six human engineering principles may seem a little complicated to begin with but actually they are not difficult at all. They will become even clearer as we study them. Once we have become accustomed to using them, we shall find that they not only give us a better understanding of ourselves, but that they constitute a whole new magic field of influencing others.

Study these six great principles, digest them and assimilate them, and most important of all, start using them now.

CHAPTER 7

SOMETHING WILL ROGERS SAID

Back in 1935 I had a privilege I shall always cherish.

I was invited to a luncheon as a guest. To my amazement and delight Will Rogers was the speaker. This was one of the last speeches Will Rogers ever made because a few weeks later he and Wiley Post started their flight around the world. We all know the tragic death they met in Alaska.

Now Mr. Rogers did not have the scholarly flavor or the academic taste that one might expect from some of the economic prognosticators of his day. But in a few words he gave some of the most profound advice I have ever heard.

I've read many books on success. I've heard dozens upon dozens of records on this same subject. But I don't believe there is a surer formula or a more certain blueprint leading to success, if followed conscientiously, than this one.

"If you want to be successful," he said, "it's just this simple.

"Know what you are doing.

"Love what you are doing.

"And believe in what you are doing.

"Yes," he said, "it's just that simple."

Now let's look into this advice a little more closely.

KNOW WHAT YOU ARE DOING

First, know what you are doing. There is no substitute for knowledge.

In our approach to knowledge we must realize that preparation is a constant process with no ending. It must be forever moving, never static. School is never out for the person who really wants to succeed. There is no saturation point. All economic research centers agree that because of the rapidly changing phases of our economy, the average person in any line of endeavor today, regardless of his particular field, must be retrained at least four times during his lifetime. Think of this:

What was not only right, but even plausible yesterday, is questionable today and might even be wrong tomorrow. It is somewhat disenchanting, I know, to find that just as we learn one role in life, we are suddenly called upon to play an entirely new part, unrehearsed, as the drama of life must go on either with us, or without us.

Knowledge is accumulating so fast and methods of doing things improving so rapidly, that a person today must run to stand still.

Up to 1900, it was said that the accumulation of knowledge doubled every century. At the end of World War II, knowledge doubled every twenty-five years. Today, all research centers tell us that the volume of knowledge in existence doubles every five years. Where does that leave the person today who thinks he can stand still and survive?

TRUE SUCCESS IS A JOURNEY, NOT A DESTINATION

The constant demands of readjustment offer a challenge today that never existed before. No longer is preparation something that can be put in a drawer and forgotten about. Success itself has taken on a new definition. It might even be termed today as the constant and continuing preparation of ourselves to meet the constant and continuing changes of our economic system. Yes, success today is a journey, not a destination.

Furthermore, in making this trip, the important thing is that we must be constantly moving forward—yes, the progressive realization of a predetermined goal. And our growth should never end. Any person who selects a goal in life which can be fully achieved, has already defined his own limitation. When we cease to grow, we begin to die.

HORIZONS OF CHANGE

One of the confusing mysteries to a child who travels along any road is that he cannot ever catch up with the horizon. None of us today can ever catch up with the horizons of change. We can only move in their direction. I am sure it is a blessing that our reach does exceed our grasp. If our ambitions in life can be fully reached, then we have not hitched our wagon to a star. We would do a great injustice to anyone if we painted the journey as being a path of roses. It is a pilgrim's road, full of obstacles and sacrifices. The only promise we can make is that if a person is willing to brave the hazards of the road, he will grow strong in the journey and keep pace with changing times.

I am sure you agree with me that regardless of how well qualified a person may be to meet the rigors of life today, if he is lulled into a sense of false security in feeling that he needs no additional preparation for the future, that his journey can ever be ended, soon he will find that he is lost in the frustrations of medieval thinking.

We have heard it said many times that there is nothing in life as powerful as an idea whose time has arrived—knowledge that is timely. If ideas are to be current and if knowledge is to be up to date, they must be forever moving, never static.

And so, first and foremost, we must embrace the principle that in order to be knowledgeable in these changing times, we must pursue a constant program of self-improvement, a never-ending journey into new fields of knowledge and learning.

A DAY OF SPECIALIZATION

Because of the rapidly accumulating volume of knowledge today, it is becoming increasingly important to specialize in some business, industry or profession. There is no escape. This, of course, doesn't mean that an individual should not be well informed in the broad fundamentals and generalities. But it does mean that in addition to this, he should to some extent be particularly knowledgeable in some aspect of his endeavors.

A rather frustrated individual the other day said, "Since we must know more and more about less and less, I guess this also means we must know less and less about more and more, which also means, pretty soon we are going to know everything about nothing and nothing about everything."

JUST HOW SPECIALIZED ARE WE?

Two fellows were talking the other day and one said, "Do you know, things are getting so specialized today that the National Biscuit Company even has a Vice-President in Charge of Fig Newtons."

The other said, "I don't believe it."

"I'll bet you," said the first.

So they put up the money and then proceeded to call the National Biscuit Company.

One said, "I want to speak to the Vice-President in Charge of Fig Newtons."

The answer came back, "Packaged or loose?"

The president of one of the largest rubber companies was recently making a speech. After he finished, the chairman opened the meeting for questions. A young man in the front row said, "Would it be too personal if I asked you how you got to be the president of this big company?"

"Not at all," was the president's reply, "I was working in a filling station and not making much progress. One day I read that if a person wanted to get ahead he must know all there was to know about his particular product.

"So, on one of my vacations I went back to the home office and watched them make rubber tires. I'd watch them put in the nylon cords. On one vacation I went to Africa to watch them plant the rubber trees and even extract the base of crude rubber.

"So that when I talked about my product, I didn't say, 'this is what I'm told,' or 'this is what I read,' or 'this is what I think.' No, I said, 'this is what I know. I was there. I watched them put those nylon cords in to make the finest tire ever made, to protect your family against blow-outs. I watched them extract that crude rubber to make the finest tire in the world.'"

He then continued, "There is no force in the world that has a greater impact than the statement of a knowledgeable person fortified by confidence and experience."

A man who knows, and knows he knows, can speak with authority that has no comparison. The world makes way for a man who knows what he's doing.

ONLY ONE WEALTH ON THIS EARTH

Lincoln once said, "The older I get the more I realize that there is but one wealth, one security, on this earth and that is found in the ability of a person to perform a task well." But he didn't stop there. He went on to say, "And first and foremost this ability must start with knowledge."

A superficial knowledge is not enough. It must be a knowledge capable of analyzing a situation quickly and making an immediate decision.

A quarterback in the closing moments of an important game called the wrong signal. A pass was intercepted and the game and conference championship were lost. That was on a Saturday. By Tuesday afternoon he had courage enough to venture out and be seen. He had to go out and get a haircut.

The barber, after a long silence, said, "I've been studying and thinking about the play you called last Saturday ever since you called it, and you know, if I had been in your shoes I don't believe

I would have called it."

The quarterback without changing expression said, "No, and if I'd had until Tuesday afternoon to think about it, I wouldn't have either."

In this modern competitive and fast moving economy of today we often don't have time to think things over and give the careful consideration to each situation which we would desire.

But still, I repeat, a superficial knowledge is not enough. Furthermore, a person who tries to substitute "gimmicks and gadgets and gizmos" for knowledge usually finds that it all boomerangs on him—he meets himself coming around the corner.

Such an attempt reminds one of the head hunter who bought himself a new boomerang. Then he spent the rest of his life trying to throw the old one away.

I feel very sorry for anyone who thinks it's possible to substitute pull or personality or any other quality for fundamental knowledge.

Yes, let's remember the sound advice of Will Rogers. If we are to be successful we must first know what we are doing.

LOVE WHAT YOU ARE DOING

But as we stated earlier in this book, knowledge, important as it is, is not enough to insure success in our complex society today. We have often heard it said, "A merely well-informed man is the most useless bore on earth."

What was Will Rogers' next statement?

Not only know what you are doing, but love what you are doing.

What are we working for? Do we love our work or are we working for money alone? If it's for money alone we are under-paid, regardless of what we are making—furthermore, that's all we shall be working for as long as we live.

Everybody loves to do business with an optimist. We can only be an optimist if we love what we are doing.

Nothing takes a greater toll on us than to be around a pessimist—a person always finding fault and criticizing others.

We've all seen the type. He has mental B.O. He's a one man grievance committee, always in session. He criticizes everyone and everything. You asked him how is business and he says, "Well, I made a sale Monday. I didn't sell anything Tuesday. Wednesday the deal I made Monday fell through—so, I guess Tuesday was really my best day."

I was recently in Boston attending a convention. I was kicked out of the hotel after two days. I thought I had a three day reservation.

As the elevator came down it stopped at the seventh floor, but nothing happened. I was irritated and in a hurry to catch an early plane and said, "Come on in."

Nothing happened.

Again I said firmly, "Come in; let's get the show on the road."

Still nothing happened.

Finally, in a loud voice, I said, "Come on in—let's go. I'll be left."

At that moment a fine looking man with a white cane, completely blind, stepped in cautiously feeling his way along.

I felt awful. I had to say something, so I cleared my throat and said, "How are you today?"

He smiled and said, "Grateful, my friend, grateful."

I couldn't say a thing—I was choked up. Any impatience or worry I had, simply shriveled into nothingness.

Here was a man blessing the darkness while I was cursing the light. I couldn't have cared less whether I caught that plane. I found myself that night in my prayers asking that some day I might see as well as that person.

Actually, each morning when we wake up if we don't find our names listed in the obituary column we should be so grateful that we are happy all day.

We can say something nice about every person or subject involved in a conversation. If not, we can at least remain silent. Nothing is *all* wrong.

Someone said that even the Black Hole of Calcutta was easy to heat.

Down in Mississippi we would say that Prohibition was horrible but that it was better than no whiskey at all.

I heard a man's name brought up the other day and someone lowered his voice and said, "Why, that fellow's a confirmed alcoholic."

The other person present said, "Well, at least, he ain't no quitter."

Let's follow Will Rogers' advice; let's constantly seek a little larger slice out of life, a few more acres of the Garden of Eden. Let's look for the happier things of existence. The great Will Rogers had the reputation of never criticizing. Why? Because he never met a man he didn't like.

BELIEVE IN WHAT YOU ARE DOING

Yes, Will Rogers said, "Know what you are doing—love what you are doing."

But he didn't stop there. He went further and said, "Believe in what you are doing."

I heard of a man who telephoned his friend and said, "Jake, I'm having a little informal birthday party tomorrow night and I want you to come to it. Come just as you are, don't stand on any ceremony. Just come right on up to the door and ring the door bell with your elbow and come right in."

The fellow said, "Well, that's all fine and good, but why my elbow?"

His friend said, "Jake, maybe you didn't understand. It's my birthday. You are not coming empty handed, are you?"

Above all else, after you finish this book I don't want you to be empty handed. If you feel amused at a few anecdotes, if you are emotionally stirred or even mentally stimulated, that's not enough.

THE ULTIMATE IN HUMAN PERSUASION

In order that you will not be empty handed, I shall give you in the next sentences the greatest principle of human persuasion that exists. There is nothing which is even a close second. If there is anything in this book that is worth remembering, it is this:

People are persuaded more by the depth of your conviction than
by the height of your logic—more by your own enthusiasm than
any proof you can offer.

If I could describe the art of persuasion in one sentence, it would be this, and I know I would be right: Persuasion is converting people—no, not to our way of thinking, but to our way of feeling and believing. And if a person's belief is sincere enough and deep enough, he is a walking climate of positive acceptance. He has an obsession that cannot be denied.

The most persuasive person in the world is the man who has a fanatical belief in an idea, a product or a service. The one common denominator of all great men in history is that they believed in what they were doing. If we could choose but one lantern to guide our footsteps over the perilous quicksands of the future, it should be the guiding light of dedication.

It has been said that words are the fingers that mold the mind of man. Words, however, can be refused. But a positive attitude that springs from a sincere belief cannot.

YOU MUST FIRST BELIEVE IN THE IDEA YOURSELF

I've heard people say in effect, "Do you believe in clairvoyance, telepathy, or psychoprediction? It's a strange thing; I knew that person was going to accept my idea the moment I walked in. Do you think I could have received thought transference?"

The answer is too obvious to need elaboration. The person presenting the idea had already made the big sale. He had bought the idea himself so completely that he was practically hypnotic in his persuasive powers.

On the other hand, I have heard a person say, "I can't explain it but I knew that fellow was not going to accept my idea even before I opened my mouth."

Of course he wasn't. The person presenting the idea didn't

believe in it and he radiated this lack of belief. He was simply admitting that he had no enthusiasm for the idea and consequently he couldn't project any enthusiasm.

Yes, I repeat, the world is a looking glass and gives back to every person a reflection of his own thoughts, beliefs and enthusiasm.

I have a picture at home that a friend painted for me. It's a picture of an old tramp sitting on a park bench. He has holes in his shoes, his knees are out and he needs a shave. His hair looks as though it had been combed with an eggbeater and he's chewing a straw. A Rolls Royce goes by driven by a chauffeur, carrying a man in a tall silk hat.

The tramp looks at it lazily and philosophically says, "There, except for me, go I."

DON'T CHAIN YOURSELF TO MEDIOCRITY

The only chains and shackles that prevent any of us from realizing our life's dreams are those we ourselves forge in the fires of doubt and hammer out on the anvil of lack of belief in what we say or do.

Will Rogers, bless his great heart, said:
"KNOW WHAT YOU ARE DOING
"LOVE WHAT YOU ARE DOING
"BELIEVE IN WHAT YOU ARE DOING"
Where can we find any directional compass in life better than this?

I know of no qualities that can be a better formula to follow—a safer directional compass—than these three great directives of Will Rogers. Study them carefully and have faith in their guiding quality. They can lead only to success.

CHAPTER 8

HUMAN ENGINEERING IS A TICKET TO ANYWHERE

As set forth in the preface of this book, one of the mysteries of mankind is that we find 20 percent of the people in practically every line of endeavor responsible for 80 percent of the constructive activities of this life and the other 80 percent responsible for the remaining 20 percent.

Why are some people creators of circumstances and others, with equal opportunity, only creatures of circumstances? Why do things happen to some people and why is it that others happen to things?

I hope this book will assist you in understanding this great mystery of life. I hope you will better realize why the human engineer finds people his opportunity rather than his problem—why, to him, life is not mystery but magic, logic and not luck.

LET'S HAVE EMPATHY

Every treatise on the subject of communication today, whether it be a book, article or record, carries something about that new plateau of understanding called empathy. I suppose its simplest meaning is an assurance that I am writing and that you are reading about the same thing—that we are in tune, that we are on the same wave length.

There is quite a difference between sympathy and empathy. For instance, let's assume that you and I are out in the ocean fishing. If you should get seasick and I said "I am sorry," that's only sympathy, but if I became green too, that would be empathy.

I once heard of a very fine example of empathy. A plumber wrote the Department of Measurements in Washington and asked the simple question, "Is it safe to put hydrochloric acid in pipe?"

He received a letter in reply as follows: "The efficacy of the method is undeniable but the precipitate corrosive residue is incompatible and conducive to metallic permanence."

The plumber studied the letter for a long time and finally wrote back, "I don't understand—all I want to know is whether I can put hydrochloric acid in pipe?"

Finally after the letter was kicked around from desk to desk it reached someone who had complete empathy with the plumber. He wrote back and said, "Don't do it, Mac, it'll eat hell out of the pipe."

I hope you and I at this point in this book are having complete empathy. I hope I am writing and you are reading about the same thing.

LET'S TAKE AN IMAGINARY JOURNEY

One Saturday night a businessman found himself in a little town in the territory he served. His car needed repairs and he couldn't drive to his home town.

The streets were bare; there was no entertainment to be found. Very bored and somewhat cynical, he walked up to a stranger on Main Street and sarcastically asked, "What is this town noted for anyway?"

The local member of the Chamber of Commerce straightened himself up and proudly said, "My friend, you can start from this town and go anywhere in the world you want to go."

I'm not sure that he was not telling the stranger off, but in any event it gives me a cue to invite you to take a little imaginary journey with me. Imagine that you have a little card in front of you. I suppose a card is made up of pulp, rags or wood and a few chemicals, but if you will just for a few minutes fill in this card mentally with me, I'll guarantee it can take you anywhere in the world you want to go—that is, if you really want to make the trip.

If you sincerely and voluntarily fill it out, it can be a ticket to take you anywhere in life; it can be a magic carpet that will take you to the great city of your dreams, aspirations and ambitions; it can be a key to open the door to the miracle of life with its wondrous possibilities. All of this is possible, however, only if you really want to make the trip.

Now, let's examine this card and fill it out carefully.

FIRST—WHAT IS OUR DESTINATION?

What is the first thing we see on any ticket? Yes, it's our destination, isn't it? Where do we really want to go in life?

Some people just don't want to go anywhere. They are bogged down in complacency and are satisfied to remain there. About all we can say for these people is that we hope they vegetate silently, unobtrusively and don't affect the lives of those around them.

JUST A SHORT TRIP

Then, we have those people who want to take just a little trip, they don't want to go very far. They want to hurry back to status quo. They have built-in limitations. They want a life of quiet desperation. They flit from mediocrity to mediocrity with enthusiasm and optimism.

As for this second group of people, all we can say is that they were born in inertia and had a relapse. They don't even burn the candle at one end. They are suffering from that scientific disease that's known in technical circles as laziness.

THEY ADVISE OTHERS IN THEIR TRAVELS

Also we have those people who don't want to take the trip, but they pose as experts on criticizing the travel of others. It's a "dog in the manger" situation. They are like the man who didn't kiss his wife for 30 years and finally shot the guy who did. They don't want to take the trip and they don't want anyone else to take the trip either.

The only thing we can say about these critics is that they were born in the objective case and have been walking around in the subjunctive mood ever since.

AS FAR AS THE TICKET WILL TAKE THEM

Finally, we have those people who want to go as far as the ticket will take them. They truly have the gift dissatisfaction and divine discontent. They have hitched their hearts to a task they love—their souls are blazing with purpose and they know where they want to go.

These people are not afraid to reach for the stars. They know that even should they miss, they'll at least not come up with a handful of mud. They'd rather shoot at something and miss than shoot at nothing and hit. They're ever conscious of the fact that there is no such thing as a trip without a destination, no such thing as success without a purpose. Ever mindful are they that obstacles are only those things we see when we take our eyes off our goal. Long ago they learned that people do not fail in this life because they plan to fail—they fail because they fail to plan.

YOUR DESTINATION MUST BE SPECIFIC

Nothing clutters up the landscape of understanding and congeals confusion as do generalities. Specifics alone give a directional compass to life.

Do you really have a specific goal in life? What is it? Is it that you want to put your kids through college? Is it to be head of your firm—president of your company?   You must have something specific you desire. If your desire is great enough, this one quality brings into focus all the other qualities within you which enable you to accomplish your specific goal.

I shall state a tragic fact. In our country, the greatest country in the world, if I went out and stopped the next two dozen people on the street, there would not be six who could recite a specific desire which governs their lives. And I am afraid there wouldn't be a dozen who could tell with certainty just why they went to work this morning.

And so the first thing we must insert in our ticket is our destination. Without this, there is no trip at all. Just as it is impossible to come back from some places we have never been, it is altogether preposterous even to suppose that we can arrive anywhere without a place to go.

Yes, we must have a destination.

SECOND—WHAT IS OUR TIME SCHEDULE?

What's the next thing we see on any ticket? It's the time schedule. When do we want to go? And more important still, when do we want to arrive at our destination? Do we want to go now, from this very room, today—this moment? Or do we want to join those disenchanted people who are always putting something off until tomorrow and consequently never take the trip?

One of the unhappy circumstances of this life is that the world is full of well-meaning but misguided people who want to prepare for the future. In fact, they periodically vow emphatically that they want success enough to do something about it, and yet somehow they never get around to it. How many of these people do you know who are always about ready to commence to begin to start to do something pretty soon.

Unless you decide to go now, I guarantee you'll never take the journey. Why? I'll tell you why. There is no tomorrow. Yesterday does not exist. We live only today, right now, this very hour. Our only existence is the present.

THE MAGIC AND MIRACLE OF TIME

Does time really have a meaning to us? Each day we have the opportunity to watch the magic and miracle of time. Time—life's most priceless tool, that which cannot be weighed in the balance or tested in the crucible. But we know it is the only ingredient that we use to transform our dreams into realities and our hopes into success.

A NEW GIFT EACH DAY

Did it ever occur to us also, that God in His infinite wisdom gives time to us in such small doses that we can't too easily squander it? Every morning, when I wake up, my pocketbook is magically filled with 24 hours of this precious, priceless substance we call time. And when tomorrow comes and I know that I have given up a whole day of my life for it, I want it to be for something that's good, not bad, some gain, not loss—something I can be proud of. And yet, Nature is so forgiving. Even if I waste it, "each night I burn the records of the day. At sunrise every soul is born again." Again I wake up—24 more of those non-refundable fragments of eternity that are magically in my pocketbook—just as valuable and unused as if I had not thrown the others away.

Did you ever hear a person say, "I just don't have time." What he is really saying is that there are other things more important to him. We all have a lot of time. We have all the time there is. The hands of the clock go around at the same rate of speed for everyone of us. The main thing is that sometimes we do not put importance on those things that are important. We give inconsequential matters disproportionate importance. Yes, we major in the minors and we minor in the majors.

THE TRIP IS NOW OR NEVER

Just how valuable is your time to you? Can you afford not to start the trip today? Our time is too valuable to waste, and since we know there is no tomorrow, then unless we fill in today's date on our ticket, I am afraid that next week, next month, next year, ten years from now, honest as may be our intentions, we shall find ourselves in the wilderness of procrastination, still responding to the siren songs of complacency.

Why can't we realize that there is no other way except by starting today? Don't we feel honestly that we are worth the investment?

STARTING NOW IS OUR ONLY INSURANCE

Most people would not drive their car from the garage unless it were fully covered by insurance. Practically everyone has insurance on his house. Very few people would dare to subject themselves to the dangers of everyday living without life insurance.

And yet insurance-minded as these people may be, many of them are not insuring their futures against constant changes by starting NOW to prepare themselves to cope with these changes.

The world owes us nothing, but we owe ourselves, our loved ones and the entire world the duty to develop our God-given qualities to the ultimate. It is a great challenge and not an easy one to meet. But it is up to us and us alone to make our dreams come true, our plans come alive.

And so, look at your ticket again. Let's make the date today—this very moment. It is the only way that we can be sure that we shall get our just share of the tasks and rewards of this life. If we don't start now, we shall never reach the great city of our ambitions and aspirations.

THIRD—WHAT IS OUR ROUTE?

What's next on our ticket? It's the route, isn't it?

Let's not be seduced by the temptation to try the easy paths of life. Some people say that the great focal point of life is where the two highways of preparation and opportunity cross. Others call it luck. I won't argue the point but this I do know. Strength always flows from adversity. Troubles, trials and sacrifices have always constituted the fertile soil for growth. If you will take time carefully to review your life, you, as does everyone else, will realize that you make your greatest progress in life during times of discouragement and challenge. You will find that the lasting qualities of life are usually forged on the anvil of disappointment.

While no one seeks hardships, yet we know that they can't be avoided along the highway leading to success. Our only choice is to meet them squarely and rise above them. The road will never be easier—it is up to us to become stronger.

AN OPTIMISTIC ROUTE

Please be sure also that you take an optimistic route. We read so much about positive thinking these days that we are tempted to be casual in considering its importance. But please never forget the sweet magic of a cheerful disposition. Everyone enjoys being around an optimist.

On the other hand a pessimist takes such a toll on us. I'd much prefer that a man steal my money than steal my optimism. The reason a pessimist is so dangerous is due to the law of emotional gravity. One pessimist can pull six optimists down with less effort than six optimists can lift up one pessimist.

Yes, we want to be kind and helpful to everyone possible, but to expose ourselves to a person with the smallpox of pessimism is a calculated risk too grave to take.

A ROUTE OF HAPPINESS

The next route is closely connected with the last one mentioned. We cannot be successful in our work or undertaking in life unless we enjoy what we are doing and feel a sense of fulfillment. Unless we are happy in what we are doing, we are a job hazard, a professional malcontent.

Years ago I was attending a convention on salesmanship.

There were six or eight small meetings going on simultaneously. One that attracted my attention was labeled "The Greatest Sale I Ever Made." I was intrigued and could hardly wait to get to the meeting. I was sure that the speaker would relate his experiences in difficult persuasion. I thought perhaps I would hear that a man ninety years old had bought a twenty-year endowment life insurance policy. Maybe, I felt, the speaker would relate the old cliché about selling two milking machines to a farmer with just one cow and then taking the cow in as a down payment.

What I really heard was this:

"The greatest sale I ever made in my life was the day I finally bought what I was doing—the day I saw the big picture, the day I had the great concept, the great passion—yes, when I truly began believing in what I was doing."

THE ROUTE OF SERVICE

We can believe in what we are doing and feel a permanent sense of fulfillment only if we know we are rendering a service to others. Any undertaking divorced from this feature has no lasting attraction. Never forget that service is the only rent we pay for the space we occupy while we are here on earth.

A person who desires to become rich should certainly not be criticized, provided he desires to become rich for the proper reason. There is certainly nothing wrong with a desire to prosper. We can do so much more for our loved ones and contribute so much more to the worth while programs in life if we are financially able. But if you are to be successful in such an undertaking, you must never lose sight of this cardinal principle: *You can never become truly rich except by enriching the lives of others; you will never truly prosper unless you bring prosperity to others.*

So, in filling out our ticket, let's not look for an easy route, but one that will make ourselves stronger. Also it should be an optimistic route and a happy route. And never lose sight of the fact that unless it is a route of service, it will lead only up a blind alley. Man is so constituted that he must feel a sense of fulfillment if life is to have any permanent meaning. Some people feel that an undertaking must be monumental and world shaking to offer a challenge. This should not be. The size of the project is of minor importance—of major importance is the unselfish effort and dedication with which we tackle the job. Remember that any place of duty, however small, is a shrine wherein we can glorify our lives with the blessings of service.

FOURTH—ARE WE WILLING TO PAY THE PRICE?

And finally at the bottom of any ticket we see this—the PRICE.

So many of us want to take the trip, but how few of us are willing to pay the price of the ticket. All of us want to improve our circumstances but how few of us are first willing to make the sacrifices to improve ourselves. I get enthusiastic over the idea of building a greater future but do I have that same enthusiasm for the slow tedious task of building myself?

I shall tell you of an incident which changed my life and which also illustrates my point. This story is related in a former book of mine. *

I was attending a college in Greenville, South Carolina, called Furman University. A professor by the name of F.P. Gaines taught me English my freshman year. He later became president of Washington and Lee University.

Dr. Gaines called on us in alphabetical order. I can repeat the entire roll call even to this day. It was important to commit the roster to memory because if you always knew just when you would be called upon, there was no need to prepare for recitation except about once each 2 months—at least that was my feeling during those green years of my life.

Furthermore, good sportsmanship demanded that if a person was sick, or absent for any other reason, he was duty bound to protect those students whose names followed his by notifying them in ample time to fortify themselves for recitation.

On a certain day when my name was fairly well up the list a very embarrassing situation presented itself. Raleigh and Riley

*The Cavett Robert Personal Development Course, Parker Publishing Company 1966.

didn't show up at class and neither one had pressed the panic button. I was unprepared, a rather normal condition under the circumstances. I had been over to a neighboring girls' college the night before to see the girl who is now the mother of my five kids.

Fortunately, however, Dr. Gaines, as he so often did, had departed from the subject of the day and was giving one of his little informational talks on some phase of personal development, which was consuming time. I have long ago forgotten the definition of a nominative predicate or the subjunctive mood. I sadly say that I am not sure I could even accurately parse a sentence. But I shall never forget some of the great inspirational ideas of life he gave us, nor will any who attended his classes ever cease to feel forever the impact of his great personality.

On this particular day, Dr. Gaines had been discussing character. Finally he picked up his roster and I knew that I was to be called on next. I glanced up at the clock and suddenly realized that the dismissal bell would ring in five minutes.

Frantically, I blundered out as I grabbed a pen and looked for a piece of paper, "Dr. Gaines, could you give us a definition of character that we could write down?"

He looked at me and then looked up at the clock as I reddened, realizing how transparent my improvised scheme had turned out to be. But he was the essence of kindness and gentleness. He looked at me and smiled. He realized, of course, that I couldn't have cared less about the definition of character.

Dr. Gaines walked around the room in silence for about a minute with his hands behind him and his chin tilted slightly upward, which was a favorite pose of his. Finally, he stopped in front of me, put his left hand on my shoulder and pointed his finger in my face.

"Young fellow," he said, "I'm not sure, but I am going to give you a definition that I want you to keep until you can find a better one."

That has been almost forty years ago and I have never heard one half as good.

"Character," he said slowly, "is the ability to carry out a good resolution long after the mood in which it was made has left you."

He continued, "Now I didn't say just the ability to carry out a good resolution. We all have our moments of supreme dedication—whether it be fidelity to a person or loyalty to an ideal. But how few of us carry out that resolution when the mood has left us and tides of temptation come sweeping in.

"Tomorrow morning, you are going to have a test on the material we have covered over the past few days.

"Tonight you will perhaps decide that you are going to get up at six o'clock in the morning and study for this test. And actually you are going to get up in the morning—that is, tonight you are, because you are in the mood.

"But tomorrow morning when you stick your foot out and it touches the cold floor you don't have that mood any longer. I say character is that which you have within yourself to substitute for the mood which has left you. Character is that which causes you to exercise the self-discipline to get up anyway."

The bell had rung but none of us had heard it. We knew it must have rung because the room was invaded by the next class.

Those five minutes have burned brightly for me over the past forty years. I would not exchange them for any entire semester of my college career.

During those forty years, on many occasions I have committed myself to some project or assignment while I was in an enthusiastic mood. I was swept along with a compulsion at the time. After the mood was gone the picture was different. The task seemed drab and difficult and without glamour or attraction. The price to pay seemed too high. On such occasions I have tried to remember this definition of character—that which we have within us to substitute for the mood after it is gone.

It is so easy to accept all parts of the ticket except the price. This is where real character and self-discipline enter the picture.

DON'T SETTLE FOR A LIMITED TRIP

Let's look at our ticket again. If we have a definite destination, if we are willing to start now, if we do not look for the easy route but for one that will make us stronger, an optimistic route, a route of service, and finally, if we are willing to pay the price, then we can with certainty know that our little ticket can take us anywhere in life we want to go. I repeat that it can be a magic carpet that will take us to the great city of our dreams, our ambitions and our aspirations. Yes, it can be a key that will open the door to the miracle of life with its limitless possibilities.

This journey is certainly not an easy trip. But human engineering is not for little people with little minds. It's not for people who are afraid the sun won't rise tomorrow. It belongs only to those brave and courageous people who dare to dream, have faith and expect the best. If you really want to take the trip, you must be willing to be baptized by immersion in some of the tougher aspects of life.

It was about two thousand years ago that a great Greek philosopher and mathematician, Archimedes, was asked if he could perform a certain task.

This is what he said: "Give me a lever that is long enough, give me a fulcrum that is strong enough and give me a place to stand, and single-handed I'll move the world."

Our lever is our goal in life. Our fulcrum is our self-discipline and willingness to pay the price. Furthermore, we must stand upon the firm ground of dedication and belief in our pursuits and activities in this life. If we have these qualities we too can move the world.

Read and re-read this chapter over and over. It has tools of greatness you cannot afford to ignore. Practice its principles and resolve to start your trip today.

CHAPTER 9

WHAT MAKES JOE GO?

It is said that an egotist talks about himself, a bore talks about others, but a brilliant conversationalist talks to you about you.

I do not claim the distinction of being a brilliant conversationalist, but I do want to concentrate for a few minutes on YOU.

My approach is going to be in the form of a question. It is one of the oldest questions that ever confronted mankind. It was old when the big stones were floated down the Nile to build the Pyramids. It wasn't new when our country was founded. Even today it is the sixty-four dollar question in the fabric of our entire economic life.

This is the question: Two people wake up in the morning in the same city; they are engaged in the same type of endeavor; all day long they are exposed to the same opportunities, tasks and rewards of this life.

One comes home that night happy, optimistic and with a feeling of fulfilled accomplishment. The other comes home disenchanted, discouraged and with a feeling of frustration.

Why the difference? They saw the same people. They walked the same streets. They offered the same service. The hands of the clock went around no faster for one than for the other.

Why is one successful and the other not? Why does one fall

into that 20 percent responsible for 80 percent of the results and
the other find himself relegated to tragic mediocrity or even failure?

If we can give a satisfactory answer to this question, we shall
in some measure answer one of the oldest questions which ever
confronted man—as old as time itself.

In offering as a solution some of the human engineering prin-
ciples, I would like to keep our approach in the form of a question.
The question is this: "WHAT MAKES JOE GO? WHAT MAKES
JOE A PRO while his colleague is a failure?"

LET'S ASK JOE

I am sure we can do no better in our search for an answer than
ask Joe himself. Let's see what Joe has to say.

Joe says, "Just lucky, I guess."

Joe tells us he is successful because he is lucky. Now let's not
be too quick in passing judgment on Joe. I am sure he is not trying
to dodge the question. He perhaps has a point.

Joe says he wants to break the word LUCKY down and explain
it to us. He asks us to sit as a jury and let him offer his evidence.
He is emphatic; however, that we reserve our verdict until he has
presented his entire case and all the evidence is in.

L STANDS FOR LOYALTY

Joe says L stands for loyalty. Yes, he says that he must be loyal
to himself, to his company and to the public he serves.

But first of all Joe feels that he must be loyal to himself. Our
first impression might be that this is a rather selfish order of
importance, but Joe feels otherwise.

Joe claims that the word "JOE" perhaps has little meaning to
other people. But to him it's the sweetest word in the English
language. It means everything in the world. He's not an egotist,
but he wants to protect that word because he knows that if he loses
it, he has nothing. He knows that he cannot be loyal to anybody
or anything until he is first loyal to himself.

Shakespeare tells us, "Who steals my purse steals trash; 'tis something, nothing; Twas mine, 'tis his, and has been slave to thousands; But he that filches from me my good name robs me of that which not enriches him, and makes me poor indeed."

Joe is resolved to preserve that name. He knows that there is a law of human engineering, an everlasting law that can never be repealed: *Public opinion is a poor tyrant compared to what a man thinks of himself.*

LOYAL TO COMPANY FOR WHICH HE WORKS

But Joe's loyalty doesn't stop with himself—it only begins there.

Joe is loyal to the company or the man for whom he works. He believes in Elbert Hubbard's statement, "If you work for a man, in heaven's name, work for him; speak well of him and stand by the institution he represents."

If you want to resign, then it is a different story. But as long as you work for a man or a company, give your very best.

LOYAL TO THE PUBLIC

Joe says we must be loyal to the public. He says that we must be a go-giver as well as a go-getter—that we can solve our own problems only through solving the problems of others.

Unless we try to do more than our share, more than is expected of us, it is a law of human nature that we end up doing less than our share, less than is expected of us. Joe says he has never yet found a statue erected to the man who stands by waiting to go through a revolving door on someone else's push.

Yes, Joe is loyal—he is loyal to himself, his company and the public he serves.

U STANDS FOR UNDERSTANDING

Joe says that the second letter in LUCKY, U, stands for UNDERSTANDING.

Joe is above all else a human engineer. He is not satisfied with just knowing WHAT a person does or even WHY he does it. Understanding in order to have any value or meaning must reveal to him HOW to cause a person to act in a predetermined manner.

As we have emphasized earlier in this book, the mastery of the third dimension, the HOW, is the most important quality in graduating into the 20 percent group responsible for 80 percent of the results. If a person ever forgets for one moment that above all else he is in the people business, if he fails to remember that knowledge or information which is not related to the problems of people is of no value, he is immediately lost in the complexities of academic theory—his productive roots are in sterile soil.

We've all heard of the surgeon who said to the young intern, "I can teach you within one hour, skillfully to remove an appendix. But it will take me four years to teach you how to cope with an emergency if something goes wrong." Yes, it would take only one hour for the WHAT, but four years for the third dimension, the HOW.

In all of our relationships with other people, let's always be mindful of the fact that we are human engineers, that we are in the people business, that we must understand the three dimensions of human engineering—the WHAT, the WHY, and the HOW.

Joe knows that if he uses only the "mumbo jumbo" in his dealings with others, he will "corn-pone" a few people into decisions he desires, but he will never know their reasons for buying or refusing. Joe assures us that U is one of the most important letters in his word, LUCKY, which he claims is responsible for success.

C IS FOR CHARACTER

Now Joe is no evangelist, he runs no revival meetings; he does not criticize the actions of others. But Joe knows this. He knows that a man cannot communicate better, he cannot convince better, he cannot do anything better until he first learns to live better. He has always known that the whole man must be developed.

Joe is careful not to be critical. If his friends want to go down to Ptomaine Tavern, they can go down every night if they choose and drink until morning. Still he doesn't criticize.

One of Joe's friends says he goes down there for just one drink. But he says that when he has that first drink it makes him feel like a new man. Then he has to buy the new man a drink. Then they must exchange drinks. Finally, his friend says by the time he gets through with the formality, the inside of his mouth tastes like a policeman's shoe and he can't work the next day.

Another of Joe's friends says he drinks only for medicinal purposes—he's sick of being sober.

Joe respects the opinions of others but he has the courage to live by his own.

K STANDS FOR KNOWLEDGE

And what does K stand for? Joe tells us that it stands for KNOWLEDGE.

We have heard of the little boy who went into the drug store and said, "Mister, can I use your telephone?"

"Sure, Johnny," was the answer.

Johnny dialed a number and said, "Hello, is this 266-2509? I want to apply for a job as a gardener. Oh! You have a gardener. Is he a good gardener? Is he doing a fine job? You have no plans to change? Well, thank you anyway."

As Johnny started out of the door, the storekeeper called him back and said, "Don't be discouraged son. That's a very commendable thing you are doing. You'll get a job, Johnny. Just keep trying."

"Who's looking for a job?" was Johnny's reply.

Rather surprised, the storekeeper said, "I am sure I heard you ask for a job as a gardener."

"Well, you see, it's this way," said Johnny rather embarrassed, "I'm the gardener—I'm just checking on my self to see how well I am doing."

How often do we play "mirror, mirror on the wall?" How often do we evaluate ourselves to make sure we are keeping pace with changing times?

Just as an experiment, ask yourself this very moment what you are doing as a result of a planned program to be sure that you are more knowledgeable in your line of endeavor than you were three months ago. How many periodicals in your field do you read each month? How many books have you read during the past year that will help you in your present work?

Joe realizes that the acquisition of knowledge is a never ending process. Being a human engineer, however, Joe is constantly increasing his "people knowledge" as well as his "product knowledge."

Y STANDS FOR YOU

And finally, Joe knows that Y stands for YOU. Joe says that success comes in a "can" and not in a "can't." Joe knows that there is but one can opener and that is YOU.

This letter in LUCKY is the very essence of human engineering—the very heart of the human equation. Joe knows that just as a book can be no greater than the author, the picture no greater than the painter, the statue no greater than the sculptor, we cannot accomplish anything greater than that which we are. Just as a physical law does not permit water to rise above its source, there is a law of nature which does not let a man's success in life rise above those qualities which are a source of this success.

One of the tragedies of this life is that many people are so much more concerned about what they OWN than about what they ARE. They would prefer having something to being something.

Joe learned early in life that what he eventually would own is only going to be a by-product of what he eventually is to be. The law of indirection taught him that if he is to build any material wealth in life, he must first start building himself.

On the wall on Joe's office hangs a framed Chinese proverb: *"Give a man a fish and he will eat for a day. But teach him how to fish and you have satisfied his hunger for life."*

GROW, THROUGH YOUR ADVERSITY

To build one's self is not an easy thing. It can't be done overnight. It's a conditioning process as well as a learning process. To prepare a person "knowledge-wise" and not condition him and develop him "people-wise" is preparing him for failure.

The development of YOU is difficult, but in the difficulty lies the opportunity. If human development were easy, then there would be less congestion at the bottom of the ladder and more at the top, which is certainly not the case today.

We grow only in the crucible of adversity. Every hardship, even every disappointment, should be the seed of a new opportunity. Did you ever analyze a little stream of water? It has no strength within itself. It is shallow and weak. But if we put a dam across it, this obstacle will cause the water to back up and get depth. This obstacle has caused the water to have strength and power. It can now generate power to drive a locomotive and it can turn the wheels of industry.

There is a law of human development similar to Parkinson's law of time. That law is this: A person's strength will grow and increase to any extent to enable him to perform the task at hand. If a person is not confronted with some great tribulation, some great challenge, Nature sees no need of wasting her resources and precious tools upon him. But if he is confronted with obstacles and resolves to overcome them, she will open up her storehouse of riches and permit him to choose whatever materials and tools necessary for him to arise to the occasion, and meet the challenge which confronts him.

Joe tells us that LUCKY not only ends with YOU but that in reality it is the determining factor of our whole existence.

And so in Joe's behalf I claim that he has proved his case to you as a jury.

LUCKY—loyalty, understanding, character, knowledge, and you—yes, the blending of these various ingredients will create something that may spell LUCKY in English. But I am sure that in the great universal language it spells SUCCESS.

CHAPTER 10

THE STREAM OF HUMAN CONSCIOUSNESS

Just as the streams and tributaries that pour their contents into a river determine the quality and flow of that river, so do the streams of influence that flow into a man's life determine his human behavior.

While this is a law as old as time itself and as definite and unchanging as the law of gravity, still we have people today who think they can violate it and escape the consequences.

The above comparison between a river and the life of man is similar in many ways, but there is one very striking difference. A river has no control over the streams that flow into it. The principle of gravitation is a cruel tyrant. Crystal clear water, muddy water, impure water from industries, waste water, sewage disposals, and any other liquid which may exist in the scope of its water shed is received without rejection.

With man it is different. Although, like the river, all that flows into his life becomes a part of him, he has the divine choice of selection. He and he alone, can determine which streams he will accept and which he will reject. He cannot accept them all because his life would be in a constant flood condition of confusion, overflowing the banks and swept along without any well-defined course. Neither can he refuse them all because soon the river of life would be completely dry. He must control the stream and direct its flow through constant selection and rejection. Let's examine a few of the streams that exist in the water sheds of us all.

EXPERIENCE VS. EXAMPLE

Many people attempt to excuse their actions and justify unwarranted conduct by thinking that they are richer by the experience. They take the attitude that unacceptable streams of events must of necessity flow into their lives in order that they can learn through experience.

We hear the expression so often, "Experience is the best teacher."

This is NOT true! We are no longer required to "muddy up" the stream of our lives in order to learn.

Human engineering has given us a whole new concept of this problem. We know now that synthetic experience, known as EXAMPLE, is a far better teacher. It is less expensive, less devastating, and gives a lasting impression to the person who learns to profit from it.

The only time experience is the best teacher is when it is the other person's experience. In our fast moving economy we do not have time to learn primarily by experience. Events move too fast; changes take place too rapidly. The emotional trauma is too great.

We are aware of the fact that most of the acceptable research centers today tell us that knowledge is accumulating so fast, and methods of doing business changing so rapidly, that the average individual in practically every line of endeavor must be re-trained four times during his lifetime. What do you think would happen to this poor fellow if he had to be retrained these four times through experience? The toll it would take on him would be too great. He would need an oxygen tent before his training was complete.

WE OVERLEARN FROM EXPERIENCE

Mark Twain once said, "If a cat sits on a hot stove he will never sit on a hot stove again; BUT, he will never sit on a cold one either."

Yes, the cat would "overlearn" from experience.

When I lived in Hog Eye, Mississippi, as a boy, my brother went to sleep on an ant hill. He swelled up and almost died. We were thirty miles from the nearest doctor. My mother jerked his clothes off and rubbed him all over with cream. Until my brother was sixteen years old, every time he saw an ant hill he jerked his clothes off. He had "overlearned" from experience.

In some of my training clinics a salesman will often go out on trial calls and make a dreadful mistake—a real "boo-boo." Unfortunately, sometimes I have had this salesman, rather than correct the mistake next time, just get out of the business altogether. The emotional trauma and embarrassment were too great for him. He fell into the trap of overlearning from experience.

The human engineer today knows that anyone who still claims that experience is the best teacher is merely voicing the echoes of by-gone days. At one time where there were very few books, records, clinics, seminars, training schools and other opportunities for study and learning, this might have been true—not so today.

Certainly we improve and perfect our methods today through constant study and use. When we cease to grow we begin to die—when we stop getting better, we stop being good. I shall always continue to keep the motto over my desk, "There's a better way to do it; FIND it." I am certainly not claiming there is any justification for the blasphemy of mediocrity. Constant improvement is the pattern for the present and, if we survive in business, it must continue to be the formula for the future.

I am saying, however, that anyone who claims today, in the light of our modern progressive training methods, that experience is the best teacher is about as practical as the man being hanged who says, "This is going to be a good lesson for me." He is about as logical as the young man who killed his mother and father in cold blood and then pleaded leniency to the Court on the basis that he was an orphan.

Furthermore, we all realize that someone must experiment in order that we gain by the experience of others. That is why so many large companies have research centers and experimental projects. Many companies spend a large part of their income on such research. Research is a profession within itself. We need "trial and error" in every business, industry and profession. However, the individual himself today is very fortunate. No longer must he be a laboratory for experimentation or a test tube to try new things. He has a seat at the head table of the benefits of research and experimentation if he will only avail himself to it. The benefits of others' experience are there for him. He cannot afford to ignore this.

TRIBUTARIES OF ENTHUSIASM

Just as we learn in geometry that the whole is the sum of the parts, we know that life's river is nothing more than the sum of the tributaries that flow into it. Some waters either pollute or purify the main stream more than others. So it is with certain influences that flow into our lives.

One of the most dominant streams of all and one that colors all other waters with which it merges is the bright stream of ENTHUSIASM. The valuable water deposits from this tributary determine the swiftness of sluggishness of the main stream. Without it, the main body of water becomes sluggish—with it, there is forever a swift and powerful flow.

Whatever may be your role in life, try also being Vice President in Charge of Enthusiasm. It pays the highest remuneration of any position you will ever hold.

Have you ever seen a person whose whole life is permeated with enthusiasm—the joy of living? He looks as though he has just rubbed the magic lamp and had all three wishes granted. You can't be in his presence without having some of his enthusiasm flow all over you—it's contagious beyond description.

This valuable tributary not only brings strength to the main stream but, just as important, it blesses and enriches any environment through which it passes.

Please don't be like the man who says, "I always feel bad when I feel good because I know I am going to feel worse pretty soon."

And I beseech you not to follow the example of the man who was so thoroughly convinced that he was going to die in the poor house that he would have his chauffeur drive him by the poor house every day to see if any more comfortable features were being added.

Anatole France said, "I prefer enthusiastic folly above complacent wisdom."

Huxley said, "The genius of life is carrying the spirit of childhood into old age."

Thoreau observed, "None are so old as those who have outlived enthusiasm."

However, there is no need to consult the minds of history's great men to realize these inevitable truths. We only need to look around us each day. We see youth at eighty and old age at thirty, depending upon the enthusiasm and zest for life which is present.

Whatever other streams fail to reach your main body of water, decide early that you will permit ample streams of enthusiasm to enter. This is a decision that cannot wait. Be sure these streams start entering your life at the head of the river. Don't wait until the river has about run its course before this precious liquid is added. Your entire life span must have the power and strength of a swift and enthusiastic current.

THE OBSTACLES THAT PREVENT THE FLOW

The human engineer is always conscious of a great law of nature and consequently he can accept it without discouragement and deal with it to his advantage. I hope it has been repeated and emphasized sufficiently in this book so that you will always remember it.

We grow strong only in the crucible of adversity. Obstacles are the only abrasive that sharpens the edge of accomplishment. We never grow until we are stretched to our ultimate capacity.

How great it would be if early in our lives we could learn to accept adversity as a blessing in disguise—if, each time we are faced with some great obstacle we realized that it is only a chance to grow—the seeds of a great opportunity.

As I look back over my life I find that those things which at the time seemed to be great obstacles and discouragements, turned out to be the most valuable things that ever came into my life. They eventually brought me happiness and fulfillment.

When once you have accepted this fact, then you are in a position to do something which truly brings magic to your life. When you are faced with some great obstacle or disappointment, instead of letting your spirits fall, simply rise to the occasion and assure yourself that something great and good will result from it. In fact, you might even speculate as to what this benefit might eventually be. Accept the fact that this is not really an obstacle but a stepping stone—not a disappointment, but a challenge. If you will form the habit of doing this, I assure you, with the depth of all sincerity I possess, that not only will you find you have an inner zest and determination to tackle the obstacle, but actually the obstacle or disappointment will already have shrunk to about half its original size before you even begin.

Man has never found any acceptable authority that states that life can ever be easier; he finds, however, everywhere, assurances of opportunities to make himself stronger to meet the challenges of life. Christianity itself was nourished in adversity and cradled in suffering. Today it is the most powerful force on earth.

GREATNESS THROUGH ADVERSITY

If we study the lives of great men carefully and unemotionally we find that, invariably, greatness was developed, tested and revealed through the darker periods of their lives. One of the largest tributaries of the RIVER OF GREATNESS is always the STREAM OF ADVERSITY.

We think of Washington in his brilliant and dramatic

moments, crossing the Delaware on ice or receiving the sword of Cornwallis at Yorktown or riding to his first inaugural with pretty girls throwing flowers in the road before him. But the essential Washington is to be found on his knees at Valley Forge with a little army, half of them sick, underfed, discouraged and cold—"flesh through the ragged blankets, purpling in the chill of a merciless frost." Behind him was a scared Congress that didn't know what to do and couldn't have done it if it had known. Before him was a far larger, well-equipped foe. At that moment this nation of ours had its sole but sufficient residence in the imperious will and the unfaltering faith of Washington—it was this Washington who is father of our country.

We see Lincoln on pennies and memorialized in the great monument at our capital city. But the inspiring fact about Lincoln is that in the 1830's he ran for the state legislature and was defeated but came back and ran again and won. In the 1840's he ran for U.S. Congress and was defeated but came back and ran again and won. In the 1850's he ran for U.S. Senate and was defeated but from that defeat he emerged so great a man that he was elevated to that eminence from which he could utter the immortal words, "With malice toward none but with charity for all."

Robert E. Lee is the abiding picture of the unperturbed Southern gentleman, but the great Lee was the Lee of 1865. He had surrendered an army in the field, and with it surrendered the nation that trusted its hopes to his mighty hand. He had lost his property, his position, his profession and even his citizenship, for he was to die five years later, still technically a paroled prisoner of war.

But he had no word of accusation for those of his own side whose better support might have brought his victory, no syllable of bitterness for those of his opponents who at times denounced him, no apology and no attempt at self-glorification or even self defense. He closed once and for all the book of yesterday and turned to tomorrow—to where tomorrows are always born, in the comradeship of youth. He turned down large financial offers from industry and became president, until his death, of the school which now bears his name, Washington and Lee University. To this school be brought the summation of his life. I repeat, it's this Lee of 1865, the Lee of adversity, who was the greatest Lee of all.

History is punctuated with instances where people became strongest at their weakest point. This is because a certain handicap to them was only a reminder and challenge to concentrate on overcoming that handicap. This is the law of the universe. If we break an iron rod at its weakest point and weld it back together again, then where do we find its strongest point to be now? The molecular fusion under heat has transformed the breaking point into the strongest point.

THE BABBLE OF THE BROOK, THE POWER BEHIND A DAM

Did it ever occur to us that without rocks and pebbles in a stream there would be no music of running water? It's the obstacles in the path of the water that cause the babbling brook. I emphasize this principle again.

If a stream is to be made useful and serviceable to man, what is the first thing to be done? The water must first be given power. Immediately an obstacle must be put in its path—a dam must be built. This principle was explained in an earlier chapter. The water is then backed up and given depth. Now the strength of its flow generates power. Factories can be operated and goods produced. The water now has begun to serve mankind. But let's remember, it could never have become useful in this manner without the obstacle in its path.

There is no need to draw the analogy with our lives. The comparison is so obvious that it needs no explanation.

I implore you to form the habit of accepting discouragements and hardships as only great opportunities. Actually greet them enthusiastically. Just as there is no physical power on this earth strong enough to hold forever a moving stream, there is no obstacle in the world strong enough and powerful enough to hold back forever the stream of your life if your tributaries keep adding the force of their contributions.

A RIVER OR A POND

The principle difference between a river and a pond is obvious to us all. The water of a river moves with an irresistible force. A pond is static—its water moves only from the force of the wind or from some other outside influence.

And so it is with people. Some move through life with an apparent self-generated force from within themselves. Others seem bogged down in inertia and move only in response to outside forces. Daily we all see examples of both.

While many people have no desire to be like a river, I am sure some of us do. We want to get ahead faster, go as far in life as we can and live as full and as enjoyable a life as possible while making the journey. Yes, some even wake up each day facing life with the passion of a lover, the fire of a crusader and the dedication of a martyr. These are the swift and powerful streams of life.

I have a cartoon on the wall of my office which clearly signifies a person who is satisfied to be a mere pond. The picture shows a tramp lying on the edge of a street gutter with a half-empty bottle in his hand. He is dirty, ragged and expressionless. He sees an expensive car go by with an immaculately dressed man driving it. He lazily glances at it and says, "I'd give a hundred dollars to be one of them there millionaires."

We know there are no bargain prices on success—no sales or discounts. We only get that for which we pay. Furthermore, not only is the price high, but we must continually be buying it over and over again.

UNIVERSAL LAW OF CHANGE

Just as a river has the quality of changing its course to conform with any change in the topography or nature of its environment, man, to survive, must also be geared for change. It is interesting to note that only those industries exist today that were imaginative and creative enough to change with changing times.

Any business that does not have, to some extent, a creative obsolescence program, is putting its future in jeopardy. The harder any company works to put itself out of business by finding new methods of doing things that will make its present methods obsolete, the greater are its chances for both survival and progress.

Please don't go the way of the "buggy-whip" companies. Examples are too numerous to mention. With the many new opportunities today, there is no reason why every company cannot keep pace with changing times and protect itself against obsolescence.

Furthermore, there seems to be no end to change. Just as the river of life is forever moving, change will never cease to flow.

I heard the president of a large electronics company recently make the statement that from now on, the imagination of one generation cannot soar to the heights of accomplishments of the next generation. As an example, he stated that Dick Tracy's comic radio watch, just a few years ago, was almost a new plateau in imagination. Today it is archaic as compared to actual accomplishment. Now, instruments the size of the watch's stem can actually do what the entire imaginative watch was said to do in the comic strip.

THE RED SEA OR THE DEAD SEA

Many writers over the years have used the difference between the Red Sea and the Dead Sea as an example in comparing two individuals.

These two seas are both fed by the fresh waters of the Jordan; they are surrounded by similar soil and enjoy the same geographical climate. However, the Dead Sea is stagnant, impure, contains no life and affects its environment adversely. On the other hand, the Red Sea is fresh, contains life and makes its entire environment a veritable paradise.

The only difference is that in the case of the Red Sea, for every drop of water that flows into it, another drop flows out. It gives with the same abundance that it receives.

Not so with the Dead Sea. It hoards every drop of water that it receives. It gives nothing and contributes nothing.

And so it is with people. If the tributaries only flow into the life of a person and none flow out, his life is stagnant—it is meaningless.

The expression, "It is only in giving that we receive" is used so often that to some it seems trite. Actually it is so fundamental that it applies to any facet of our personal and business existence.

Unfortunately, very few people feel the desire to give back something in return for that which they receive! We have a famine today in appreciation. To some, appreciation means only anticipated favors yet to come. To others it is a humble gratitude for the consideration of others.

CHOOSE A DEFINITE COURSE AND FOLLOW IT

Any river that is not following a definite course is in flood condition and destroys rather than enriches. It is off-course.

Any individual who does not follow a predetermined course in life is dissipating his energies and wasting his efforts. Nothing useful is ever accomplished.

The task of sticking to a set course in life is difficult for some people. It is their reason for failure. Maybe they have ability, personality and energy. These mean nothing to a person who is off-course. He has about as much chance of accomplishing anything as has a hen who is trying to hatch twenty different nests of eggs, running from one to the other.

When a person has finally learned to follow conscientiously a prescribed course of action, it is amazing how the complex becomes simple to him and the mysterious becomes plain.

Theodore Roosevelt once said, "I am only an average man but, by George, I work at it harder than the average man." He then went on to elucidate further by saying that he selected one course of action and simply stuck to it. This is good advice for us all.

And so, as we close this chapter on the various streams that flow into our lives, let's remember that these tributaries mean nothing unless the main river stays on course. Periodically, in a judicious way, we should examine our lives and take every precaution never to get off-course. If we find ourselves straying from the prescribed channel, we should make every effort to return as quickly as possible.

Take a "think break" and examine your own life. Make a list of those tributaries that are adding strength, happiness and growth. See if there are some which should be eliminated. The choice is yours. We, and we alone, control the flow into the great River of Life.

CHAPTER 11

POSITIVE MORALITY

There is a great constructive force which is apparent in every aspect of a truly successful person's life. It can best be described as POSITIVE MORALITY.

Positive morality connotes a compelling desire for good to do rather than finding satisfaction in avoiding the obvious evils. It is not limited in scope to the spiritual life of a person. It applies equally well in every walk of life—in his business, his social and his civic exposures.

The human engineer knows full well that unless the same truth applies equally to every facet of his existence, it is not truly a principle of life. We have held to the philosophy throughout this book that truth is a whole and fragmentation an error. Do you know of anyone who has a truly successful life in one field of activity and utter failure in another? There may be appearances of temporary accomplishment but no lasting success. Nature has a way of letting her well-deserved blessings flow from one compartment of a person's life into all compartments to enrich his whole existence.

SEE NO EVIL, HEAR NO EVIL, SPEAK NO EVIL

All of us have seen the three little statues, depicting an ancient and discarded morality. Hands are over the eyes, over the ears and over the mouth. The philosophy portrayed is that good is found in not doing evil. This is a completely negative approach to life. What kind of society would we have, how progressive would be our economy if the highest standard of performance had its foundation in negative morality?

Theodore Roosevelt described this positive morality beautifully when he praised the man of energy and certainty of purpose who forever was striving to meet higher standards:

"The credit goes to the man who is actually in the arena—whose face is smeared with sweat and dirt and blood—who at his best knows in the end the triumph of high achievement and who at his worst at least failed while daring greatly—so that his name shall never be among those cold and timid souls who know neither defeat nor victory."

There has never been a man of greatness, there has never been a contribution to this world through any activities that did not have their origin in positive morality.

DOING RIGHT FOR THE WRONG REASON

I have always been amused at the expression that a person should never try to give good advice until he is too old to set a bad example. While I am not one of these weak individuals who yield to the temptation of depriving themselves of a pleasure, I also am no admirer of a "reformed reprobate by necessity." I have never yet met a "Man of Distinction" who was elected to this honor because of sins he didn't commit or errors he didn't make. Also, I have visited many art galleries and never yet have I found a statue to commemorate a person who did the right thing for the wrong reason.

SCHIZOPHRENIC MORALITY

All of us have had occasion to know people who suffer from schizophrenic morality. They are church goers and pay great lip service to right doing. However, when the expediency of the moment demands, they pigeon-hole their religion and have open season on their fellow man. They melt the "golden rule" and mold the "golden calf."

We had such a character in a little town where I lived as a youngster. He was the first man at church each Sunday morning and Sunday night in order that he could claim his seat on the AMEN row. He held his head the highest when he sang and bowed his head the lowest when he prayed.

This was all fine and good except for the fact that he spent practically all the remaining part of the week in the county jail for drunkenness, disorderly conduct and other sins of the disposition.

At one of the numerous revival meetings that were held in our little town, I remember so well, even unto this day, the very strange testimony he gave in a loud sanctimonious voice as he stood up from his front row seat in a spirit of confession and said in substance,

"I'm not the best man in town, as you all know. I have done my share of drinking and gambling. I have a bad temper that I can't control, which leads to fights, even with some of my friends. I spend more time in jail than I would like to. But in spite of all these things I am proud to say that at no time have I ever lost my religion."

TRY TO DO OR TRY NOT TO DO

Let's remember this fact: *A constructive life is built of the things we do—not of the things we don't do.*

I once heard a person who was being criticized make the remark, "I know my way is not perfect but I like the way I do it better than the way you don't do it." Never forget that the only material which can be used in building a life is positive action. Negative inaction is valueless in constructing anything except criticisms and excuses.

Some people who do not understand positive morality spend

so much time and energy trying to refrain from error that they are too tired for positive accomplishments.

Perhaps most of us have heard of the little boy who nervously was hanging around the apple barrel in the country store.

Finally the owner said, "Johnny, are you trying to steal one of my apples?"

"No," Johnny said, "to be truthful with you, sir, I am trying not to steal one."

LET IT START WITH ME

Positive morality, if it is to be of any value to any of us, must start with one's self.

It certainly does not have its beginning in criticizing the other person because of his faults. It must commence with serious and voluntary self-analysis. There is an old church hymn I sang as a child which started thus, "Dear Lord, send us a revival and let it start with me."

At a recent convention which I was attending I had occasion to hear a speech entitled, *"Who is to blame?"*

I was sitting next to a salesman who remarked to me that he was sure his sales manager's face was red.

An hour later I was talking to the sales manager about the speech and he confidentially told me that if that speech didn't jar the vice-president in charge of marketing nothing would.

I sat next to the vice-president at the banquet that night and I asked him what he thought of the speech. His only remark was that he would have given a month's salary if the president of the company could have heard it. He said that he was sure it would have straightened a few things out.

The speech had many good qualities about it but it had fallen on deaf ears. Not a person I met had accepted it as anything to do with himself.

Positive morality is a personalized morality. It is not born of criticism—only self-analysis. Criticism is a very cheap thing but no one yet has ever had the price to buy it back.

THE LAW OF EXPANSION

Positive morality has its very foundation in the law of expansion. It is only by using those qualities which we already possess that we shall have other qualities in greater abundance.

This was the very essence of the Parable of the Talents. It is the story of Elijah and the handful of meal and bit of oil possessed by the widow. The prophet knew that if he could get the widow to put her meager possessions into circulation, into use, the law of expansion would bring about a miracle.

Why do some of us try to use this expansion principle in reverse? We expect our possessions to increase and multiply when we haven't even put into circulation that which we already have.

Have you ever observed a person who became frightened of his business future and who committed economic suicide by trying to correct the situation through a reversal use of the law of expansion? By expansion we do not necessarily mean increasing the size of one's business. We mean using to a greater extent the present facilities which one already owns. This applies both to individuals and to companies.

Positive morality is the principle of using, in an active and positive way and to the fullest extent, all the tools of success we possess. If I wanted my arms or legs to be stronger, I would use them to a greater extent each day, requiring more of them progressively. If, however, I committed them to non-use in order to save them, they would wither and soon become useless. This same principle holds true in every field of endeavor.

POSITIVE MORALITY DEFINED

Webster describes POSITIVE as "admitting of no doubt." He describes MORALITY as "fundamental truths of human conduct."

Then we can say with certainty that positive morality is interpreted as "fundamental truths of human conduct, admitting of no doubt."

It is important to note from this definition that POSITIVE

MORALITY is not limited to "positive thinking." Added are two very important qualities, "conduct" and "fundamental truths." And so, positive morality is a combination of "positive thinking," "positive action" and "integrity."

The twentieth century is generous with its great men of positive thinking. The little Frenchman Coué was one of the first. So challenging was his philosophy that many people would greet each other on the street with the salutation, "Day by day in every way, I am getting better and better."

We were practically hypnotized by the philosophy that we can change our circumstances in life merely by changing our own thinking.

Others warned us to beware of what we wanted and wished for because we would get it.

Still others told us that whether we thought we could or whether we thought we couldn't, we were right.

None of this very fine philosophy is new. It is simply old wine in new bottles.

The best source of all is the Holy Bible itself. Almost two thousand years ago we were told that as a man thinketh in his heart, so is he.

START WITH POSITIVE ACTION TODAY

The various philosophies of positive thinking are wonderful, but miracles can be precipitated only if the catalyst, positive action, is added. When we combine positive thinking with positive action, then we are approaching positive morality.

I have a friend in Florida who now builds his life around positive morality. I believe his library contains every book which has the positive approach to life's problems.

He told me that at one time he would get up every morning, stand before the window, take a few deep breaths of fresh air and say, "This is the greatest day of my life. I know something good is going to happen today."

He explained that this turned out to be a fine way to recharge the batteries of positive thinking and rekindle the fires of energy. However, he said it was not until later that he began experiencing any positive results.

This happened only after he changed his morning recitation. Now, he states with all the depth of sincerity he possesses, "This is the greatest day of my life. I know something good is going to happen today BECAUSE I AM GOING OUT AND GOING TO MAKE IT HAPPEN."

My friend at one time received great confidence from assuring himself each morning, "This is the first day of the rest of my life."

He confessed to me that the statement had no power of accomplishment until he changed it to, "This is the first day of the rest of my life and *I am going to make it one of the best.*"

The thoughts and ideas contained in this chapter can influence your life for growth and security. Take positive thinking and positive action and combine them, along with integrity, into positive morality. Let this great human engineering principle act as a directional compass in your business, social, civic and personal life. If you do so, you will find that miracles do still happen.

CHAPTER 12

THE CREDENTIALS OF LEADERSHIP

Newspapers, radio stations and television stations, I am told, receive more requests for favors from the public than any other industries. Perhaps it is because their exposure is the greatest.

Recently I read of a request made to one of the major radio networks by an old sheepherder out in Idaho. He lived all alone, miles away from any other people. His letter in substance was as follows:

"I look forward to your program every Saturday night and enjoy it very much. I want to ask a favor of you. About the only entertainment I have, besides listening to your program, is playing my old violin. It has gotten so badly out of tune lately that I can't play it. Now I wonder if you would be kind enough next week to stop your program and strike an "A" note on the piano several times so I can tune my violin and start playing again?"

After the unusual letter made the rounds of a few desks and got many laughs, it was promptly filed in the waste paper basket. The story circulated throughout the company and by chance the president heard of it.

To the astonishment of many, the president said, "Why

shouldn't we grant the man's request? He is one of our listeners. We are here to serve people and here is a fellow who needs help."

A week later the sheepherder wrote again thanking the station and assuring those in charge that his violin was now in perfect tune and that he was enjoying it again.

I know nothing about this president or his company, but I am sure of one thing. He is a person blessed with one of the most important credentials of greatness. He has a sacred respect for SERVICE.

Above all else, a true executive is service minded. To serve is the ultimate concern of every business—the final goal. Sometimes, however, a busy executive becomes so involved in means, methods and tools, that he forgets end results.

If the chief executive forgets it, then this imbalance of emphasis permeates all too quickly throughout the entire organization. We cannot ignore the fact that the head of any company is in truth the mainspring and the fountainhead from which all policies stem.

I once knew the head of a large utility company who never let a single employee forget that first and foremost he worked for a service company. He constantly reminded the meter readers that while they were responsible for reading meters, this was only incidental to serving the public. He went out personally to converse with linemen stringing wire. This popular man, in a very tasteful way, would not let the linemen forget why they were stringing wire—so that the public could be served. The engineers, repairmen, accountants and all others received the same admonition. It is needless to tell you that this company built a great image of service in every city where it operated.

HANDLING THINGS VS. HANDLING PEOPLE

If a person is to rise to any position of responsibility in life, he must embrace this principle of human engineering and never forget it: WE GET THINGS DONE THROUGH PEOPLE. It is not enough to be good with things; we must be good with people.

One of the biggest fallacies today in promoting people to positions of importance is our belief that their proven excellence in dealing with things will also apply in the field of dealing with people. This is a costly mistake and one made much too often today. Some companies even reward employees by giving them higher positions because of past performance without properly evaluating their ability to cope with personal problems that might be involved in the new assignment.

As any person rises higher in a company, more and more time must be spent in managing people and less and less time in managing things.

For instance, let's imagine that I am a repairman for a large truck delivery company. I prove to be a great mechanic and am promoted to supervisor of the entire repair department. Unless I understand the transition from dealing with inanimate things to supervising people, I might think my new position is to be in charge of all repairs. In reality, my new responsibility is to work through people in satisfying the needs of that department.

Unless a company realizes that there is not necessarily any connection between the ability to handle things and the ability to handle people, great harm can be done both to the company and to deserving employees.

I have in mind a very unfortunate case where an excellent engineer for an ice company was promoted, because of past performance and years of service, to chief engineer of the company. Although he was a fine mechanical engineer, he did not know, and did not seem to be able to learn, the first principles about human engineering. His success at his old job was exceeded only by his failure at his new position. Completely unable to cope with his new assignment, he was sent back to his old job where he had once been completely happy and satisfied. The humiliation of being demoted completely broke his spirit and he finally left the company.

This tragic experience was due to no fault of the man, but was due to the bad judgment of those who promoted him without a proper evaluation of his ability to meet the job requirements. This, unfortunately, is not an isolated case. It happens too frequently in our business world today.

DELEGATING AUTHORITY

If I were required to name the credentials of leadership in the order of their importance, I'm sure I would put the ability to delegate responsibility at the very top. More executives fail because of their inability in this field, than for any other reason. Actually, a great deal of research has been done on delegating responsibilities and there is a wealth of information on the subject. One of the first things a person should do, when he is newly elevated to a position of authority, is to make an exhaustive study of the field of delegation.

Any intelligent approach to this important subject requires that we relate it to three dimensions of human engineering. First, let's consider WHAT we delegate, then WHY we delegate and, finally, most important of all, HOW we delegate.

WHAT TO DELEGATE

Since we define delegation as "permitting one's subordinates to make decisions under certain circumstances without consulting you, taking action without asking you (just keeping you informed), and being given the security of a certain amount of authority and backing while doing it," we must first examine certain responsibilities to see which ones lend themselves to such delegation.

If you were promoted to a position of responsibility that required delegation, I would suggest first of all that you carefully list all the responsibilities of your department or position. You would find that some are in the field of policy making and some are more routine. Some are so important that an error in judgment or in handling would cause much damage; others, if handled improperly would not affect overall results materially. Some duties are easily handled and can be grasped quickly. Others are more intricate and require much study and training.

Next, you must study the background, abilities, and experience of those employees for whom you are responsible. It would be of little value to you to understand the nature of tasks to assign if, at the same time, you did not understand the qualifications of those who are to accept these responsibilities.

Sometimes you will even find that there are certain responsibilities which should be assigned, but, at the time, you do not have qualified employees who can accept such responsibilities.

A successful department head is constantly upgrading his employees through training so that he can delegate more and more responsibilities.

And so in determining WHAT to delegate, we must understand both job requirements and the abilities of employees. One without the other is not enough. Both require constant study and understanding. Both are variables and may change from time to time.

The more an executive can delegate with safety, the more valuable that executive is to his company. It is about the best recommendation that a person can receive. If a supervisor only delegates routine and unimportant duties over a period of time, when actually there are more important tasks that could be delegated, he is not a leader and the situation should be rectified in some manner.

WHY WE DELEGATE

About the worst recommendation that can be said for any department head is to say that his department is a *one man department.* Not much would be accomplished if a person tried to do everything himself. The responsibility is not to do the work himself, but to get the work done through other people.

And so the first reason that one delegates is that only through delegation can one get the required amount of work done. Show me a department where the supervisor tries to do more work individually than he should do and I'll show you a department subject to "bottlenecks," panics and constant crises.

When we discover such a situation as this, we usually also find a supervisor who enjoys power and finds satisfaction in exercising authority, meeting emergencies and fighting management fires.

If an executive can effectively delegate, he is released from certain responsibilities and consequently has more time to improve and, when necessary, expand his department. If a supervisor is overloaded, he does not have an opportunity to train properly or to devote himself to problems which need immediate attention.

Many employees suffer from job monotony. The best cure for this is a feeling of responsibility. A feeling of responsibility goes hand in hand with initiative, motivation and employee morale.

It should be the goal of every supervisor to delegate responsibility and develop his department to the position where it can run smoothly without him for a reasonable time. Of necessity, there are occasions, such as sickness, vacations, training courses and the like when the supervisor must be away. During this time, he should feel a sense of security, that all is well while he is absent. The degree to which this is possible is a reflection of the supervisor's ability to delegate properly.

Many a supervisor has lost the opportunity of a valuable promotion because he has not attempted, through delegation of responsibility, to develop a person who could immediately step into his shoes in the event of a vacancy.

I know the president of a large corporation who climbed through every plateau of responsibility on his way up. From a new employee he went to "straw boss," foreman, supervisor, general superintendent, etc. I asked this president if he could put his finger on any one factor which contributed to his rise more than anything else.

His answer was very interesting. He said that after assuming each new position, he set about trying to fire himself—trying to train a man who could do his job better than he himself could do it. This is the very highest dimension of delegation.

WHY PEOPLE DON'T DELEGATE

One of the principle reasons some people don't delegate is an innate feeling of insecurity. They are afraid that if someone else can handle their job, they are no longer needed. Such reasoning is colossal insanity—nothing is further from the truth. Actually, they are available for a promotion. If a supervisor should ever feel insecure, it is when he does not have anyone who can step into his shoes.

Some people don't have the capacity of being able to put confidence in other people. The inability to trust and believe in the other person is a very serious fault. Unless this can be overcome, a person is not a fit candidate for a supervisory position. Without this confidence he will never be able to delegate.

Many supervisors are handicapped in delegation because they do not know how to train a person to accept and carry out the responsibilities delegated. A supervisor may be proficient in the work of his department but unless he can impart his knowledge to others, his ability to delegate is greatly limited.

We have heard the expression many times, "If the employee hasn't learned, the supervisor hasn't taught." While this is an old axiom, it should not be treated lightly.

HOW TO DELEGATE

Now we come to the third dimension of delegation, HOW to delegate.

When you approach an employee about accepting a new task, by all means present it to him as a challenge, as an opportunity, not as just another chore.

"Bill, this is an important job, one that has to be done quickly. I believe you are the fellow who can do it. Do you think you can?"

The supervisor who can get an employee excited over a new responsibility has learned a great lesson in delegation.

The supervisor who knows the human engineering approach is careful to see that an employee does not look upon a new task as a risk of failure. Rather he challenges him to accept it as an opportunity for success.

A person, in delegating jobs, should never overlook the fact that the task is more interesting to the employee if it has the element of teamwork connected with it. It gives an employee a sense of security to know that others are working on the project with him. There is the added factor that each feels he must do his share so that the others are not let down.

An extremely effective way of delegating responsibility is through discussion with the employee. Instead of telling him, ask him questions. Get his recommendations.

"Bill, an important job has just come up. How do you feel it ought to be handled?"

If he tells you, then you have HIM involved. This is HIS way. Also, you can bet that he wants to prove that he was right, and he will do a good job. You have his ego at stake.

When you delegate, you will find that the employee is usually much more receptive if you delegate a complete package; that is, a project or finished job. If the employee can visualize a completed task, he feels the opportunity for fulfillment—otherwise, it is merely putting in just so many hours on a routine basis. This may seem trivial, but to the employee, it may be the difference between boredom and a challenge.

MAKE YOURSELF UNDERSTOOD

Regardless of what method you use in delegating responsibility, be sure that you make yourself clear—be sure that the employee understands fully. There is only one way that you can do this and that is by asking questions.

"Let's see, Bill, are we clear on this point? How was it that we felt this part of the work should be done?"

In asking questions, it is preferable to ask the question in such a way that the employee must recite some of the details in his answer. This is one of the best ways to insure that he fully understands.

"Just to make sure that you and I are together in our understanding, Jim, repeat back to me your view of what is to be done."

SET UP CONTROLS

If you want to be sure that your instructions are going to be carried out, mere delegation is not enough. You must set up controls. Have the employee report back to you. Be sure he gives you progress reports.

"Let's see now, Charlie, will you report back to me at ten o'clock tomorrow morning on how things are progressing? You see, they will be here at three tomorrow afternoon to pour the cement."

Now you have given yourself some protective time. If for some reason Charlie is not far enough along to suit you, you at least have time to put an emergency squad on the job and get it done.

The certain way of flirting with disaster is to delegate responsibilities and then forget about it. You must inspect the work or get progress reports to be sure the work will be completed in the prescribed time. The old axiom still holds true, "We get what we INSPECT, not what we EXPECT."

PARTNERSHIP RESPONSIBILITY

One of the best methods of getting the utmost from those you supervise, is to make them feel that you are WITH them rather than OVER them. I don't mean that you should ever abdicate any of your authority. Employees like to feel that their supervisor is both firm and fair. I do mean, however, that you should make the employee realize that his success is your success and his failure is your failure.

If an employee performs a poor job and you jump all over him and bless him out, what do you think would be his reaction?

If, on the other hand, you said, "Bill, I think that you and I together can improve on this job. Let's see what we can do. Why don't you try it again?"

Bill feels a part of something. Poor work is a reflection not only on himself but on the department and on you. I am sure he will try harder.

When I worked in a large New York Wall Street law firm, for six months I was strictly in what was called the Research Department. I would write memoranda of law on various points for two of the senior partners who were trial lawyers. The first time I delivered a memorandum to one of these men, he took it and then said, "All I want to know, Cavett, is this the best that you and I together can do?"

The remark scared me. Immediately I felt that my standard of performance must be of a quality worthy of a senior partner. It suddenly dawned on me that if that memorandum was not correct in all respects, it would be a reflection on the top men of the law firm. Momentarily I felt a partnership responsibility with him.

Fortunately I knew that the law contained in the memorandum was correct. I had checked it and rechecked it. From that moment, however, I felt a much greater responsibility and I tried even harder the next time I received an assignment.

EMPLOYEES LIKE TO BE CONSULTED

One of the outstanding qualities of a great leader is the ability to make an employee feel important. Furthermore, one of the greatest ego builders to an employee is to have his supervisor ask for his opinion on something.

But merely to ask an employee questions is not enough. His opinion must be sought out in a sincere manner and the supervisor must be a good listener.

ASK WINDOW QUESTIONS, NOT MIRROR QUESTIONS

If you are sincere in wanting to know what an employee's real opinion is, don't try to influence him in your questioning.

Don't say, "This is the way I see it, Mack; isn't that about the way it appears to you?"

This is a "mirror question." You can't begin to get even a suggestion of his real opinion. Furthermore, it is evident that you have already made up your mind. You have no desire to know how he feels about it and even if he gave you his opinion, he is certain that your mind is closed.

Rather than the above, try a "window question."

"Mack, I'd like to get your ideas about this problem. You are closer to it than anyone else."

"That sounds interesting, Mack; do you mind telling me in detail just why you feel that way about it?"

Now Mack is convinced that you really want to know his opinion. You have let him feel that his opinion is valuable to you. Undoubtedly he will open up under these conditions just as fully as he would have closed up under the first approach.

Not only is this good human engineering if done sincerely, but you actually will profit a great deal from the opinion of your employees. They are on the firing line close to the problems and often have an insight into problems you might have overlooked.

HOW TO MAKE A DECISION

There are very few subjects in our present economic field which have received as much attention or had more words written about them than the subject of *Making Decisions*. This is as it should be because no business, industry or profession can operate divorced from decisions.

The head of any company, department or project is always faced with the responsibility of making decisions. If the decision is completely covered by company procedures or policies, the decision is merely an administrative act. In the majority of cases, however, this is not true. Consequently, it is helpful to the person in authority to have a certain formula or pattern to follow as a guide line in his decision making.

GET THE FACTS

If there is one over-all principle that applies in every case where decisions are concerned, it is this: *No one's judgment is any better than the facts on which it is based.*

Until we have gathered all the available facts, we do not even know what the exact problem is. Just how much information we should accumulate is determined by the importance of the problem and how much time we have before action must be taken.

If the problem is a small one, it would obviously be illogical to spend a large amount of money and time assembling facts. On the other hand, if the problem is critical, the case may be otherwise. Remember this in determining the number of facts necessary: Many have made the wrong decision because of an insufficiency of facts; no one has ever made the wrong decision because of too many facts.

In assembling facts, the information should be screened carefully. We must be particularly careful in trying to ascertain the real problem, that we do not confuse opinions, prejudices and biased statements with actual facts.

When we are satisfied that we have defined the exact problem, we should weigh it carefully before taking the next step. It may be that it is so incidental, once brought to light, that actually a problem does not exist. It may be that it is the type of problem best solved by time and no action should be taken. Even in some instances it may be that for some reason no action CAN be taken. There are exceptional cases, however.

CONSIDER POSSIBLE COURSES OF ACTION

After we have accumulated all the available facts and feel that we can see the real problem, we must consider the possible choices we can make.

Even if one course of action seems obviously best, at least explore and consider all possible avenues of decision. If you eventually decide on the first course, you will be even more convinced that this is the best choice if other courses have been carefully weighed.

Review the various courses before making a final decision. Be sure that you have considered each unemotionally and that bias or prejudice has not entered into your consideration.

DECIDE ON ONE COURSE AND ACT

In selecting the one course of action, there are obviously many things to consider. A few of the more important are as follows:

Does this course offer a real solution or does it merely delay or sidestep the problem?

Can we find any precedent for such a course? If not, can we test the course before going ahead completely?

How expensive will this course be?

Will it violate any company policies or set any dangerous precedents?

Have we sufficient personnel to carry through?

Although it may solve the present problem, will it create any new ones?

Will it affect the over-all picture in any adverse way?

Even though there may be several courses equally desirable, we must eventually choose one course and ACT. No decision is really a final decision until action takes place. Until then, it is merely academic theory.

All decisions have an element of risk involved. This risk, however, can be mitigated through a proper follow up program.

Be sure that the decision is put into effect fully and carried out with precision. If the decision affects employees, be sure all are informed of the action and be ready to answer questions where necessary.

If you find that you did not have all the facts, or that the facts have changed, have the courage to withdraw the decision and make a new decision in the light of true facts. Keep all who might be affected informed of your new action. Don't continue with an erroneous decision just to save face.

START BEING A LEADER TODAY

The real work of a person's life on this earth is determined more than anything else by the things he writes indelibly and the things he engraves deeply in the lives of others. No one has the opportunity to write so indelibly or engrave so deeply as the person who supervises others in their work. Of all the arts on this earth, none is so valuable as the art of building people.

In order to be a leader of men, the supervisor must be truly interested in his employees. He must actually like them, be interested in their welfare and all that concerns them. The employees can easily determine whether the interest is faked or genuine.

A good supervisor accepts the blame for any failure that takes place in his department. He never passes the buck or tries to side-step criticism directed toward his department. Realizing this, his employees have an added incentive to prevent mistakes that would cause embarrassment to their supervisor.

The supervisor goes to bat for those in his department. He doesn't just tell his employees that he has their interest at heart. He proves it. Under normal circumstances he will stand up for an employee when attacked from another department of the company, though he may later "set straight" his employee in private. He never praises his employees insincerely nor does he criticize them unjustly. His prime concern is to be fair and impartial with them at all times. His employees are never afraid to go to him with their troubles. They realize he will listen with sincere interest.

It is not easy to be a leader. As was emphasized earlier, many can learn to manage things but only a few become proficient in managing people. This calls for constant study of the principles of human engineering and motivation. But to a leader who has taught others to live more abundantly, the rewards are great—the fulfillment is without comparison.

Chapter 13

A New Dimension in Recruiting

The most vital factor in the growth or survival of any business or industry today is its personnel.

Usually a company's credit rating is judged by its balance sheet and periodic financial reports. However, its true potential performance rating is not to be found there. It's contained in its personnel.

We know full well and have pointed out elsewhere in this book, that if every vestige of the physical assets of a company were suddenly destroyed, in most instances the company would find a way to recapitalize itself and would soon be doing business as usual. However, if the entire personnel of this same company were wiped out, there would be little chance of its survival. Yes, manpower, although it does not appear in the balance sheet, is the one indispensable factor of every company.

Our freshman football coach in college, in his efforts to get us to use self-discipline and keep training, had a great saying which he repeated many times during the season: "The acid test of any football team is the character of the men who play the game."

I am sure this is not restricted just to a football team. It has a universal connotation. In particular, does it apply to the personnel of a company. There is no factor of greater importance.

PERSONNEL FIRST IN IMPORTANCE

It was not too many years ago that about the total function of personnel was contained in the few expressions "hiring and firing," "filling vacancies," "stepping a man up," or "stepping him down." We never had a personnel department, only an employment office.

The dignity of man and the worth of the individual have traveled far since this archaic doctrine was discarded. Personnel policies are now given major consideration by all progressive companies.

Sir Isaac Newton revolutionized the field of physics when he expounded the formula: *Mass times acceleration equals force.*

The distilled experience of many years has finally caused us to recognize an economic law just as profound: *Product or service times qualified personnel equals profit.* This law cannot be ignored or defied any more than a physical law, without disastrous effects.

HUMAN ENGINEERING DEPENDS ON ENGINEERS

Yet, in spite of the trend toward acceptance of the importance of personnel, some companies are loath to be progressive in this direction.

They will spend vast amounts on physical facilities just to make their premises impressive; they will go the limit in providing the most modern equipment known to the genius of invention; they will employ the finest architects, engineers, accountants and lawyers. But when it comes to assembling and training employees to justify these expenses and make its operations productive, these companies are unwilling to spend the time and money necessary.

Without a dynamic, progressive personnel to breathe life into their inanimate equipment, regardless of the value of the physical equipment, a company has nothing except a spreading, malignant, cancerous overhead and is faced with trouble in the future. While we are certain that human engineering is the magic ingredient which will give this life, we are just as certain that there will be no human engineering unless we first assemble and train the human engineers.

WHAT IS THE ANSWER?

You might say, "Don't keep screaming about the problem. Let's look toward the third dimension in human engineering. Let's consider HOW to tackle the problem. Answers are what we all are after."

I fully agree with you. But in many instances, subconsciously, we know the problem and are not willing to acknowledge it simply because we are not sure we have the courage to tackle the solution. Until we have definitely, unequivocally and openly proclaimed manpower as the number one problem of our economic life today, we cannot be helped any more than can an alcoholic who is unwilling to confess his problem.

Any owner, or anyone responsible to ownership of a new company, who does not openly acknowledge that his major problem is to develop a dedicated and stable group of employees, is either mentally dishonest or so ignorant of his problems that he is going to fail anyway.

When a company head tells me that he has no personnel problems, I always recall the statement of a philosophical old Arizona rancher who once said, "I hate to have a man tell me that he is boss of his wife because if a man will lie about one thing he will lie about everything."

WHO IS RESPONSIBLE FOR RESULTS?

The ultimate aim of every company is to get results and render a service to the public by having its product or service accepted. To be successful in this regard, a company must go to the stream's head and concentrate on that which is responsible for results. We, of course, know that successful results flow only from a successful personnel.

And so regardless of how desperate we may be for manpower,

regardless of how great the personnel emergency may be, if we try to take short cuts in this regard, we are creating problems rather than solving them—we are flirting with disaster.

Naturally an organization under some circumstances must have an accelerated program of recruiting and training, but it must not sacrifice the immediate for the ultimate. It must not let quality and thoroughness suffer because of numbers.

Many of us have had occasion to observe a "crash program" of recruiting and training to meet some dire emergency. People were employed because they were *available* rather than because they were *qualified*. Such a method as this invariably invites trouble. The usual "hit and run" employees are on the scene, looking for advances, "rocking chair money," and everything else they can get. The mortality rate is high and we find that we are distilling a gallon to get a drop.

THE IDEAL EMPLOYEE

Not long ago I took part in a very exhaustive study in the field of human engineering to determine just what are the qualities of an individual that give him job stability so that there is a curtailment of the centrifugal force that causes him to fly off in all directions as soon as the wheels of production begin spinning.

The study revealed nothing that all of us didn't already know. These people were dedicated to their work, were disciples of positive thinking, had good work habits and followed a constant study and learning program. We certainly have no difficulty in determining the kind of person we want. The real problem is in determining the method of enlisting this person's services.

HOW DO YOU ATTRACT HIM?

I continued my study of this subject into the experimental field. We all know that the usual methods of recruiting bring SOME results. We find people who want to change jobs, some who are looking for their first job, and some who have just come into a new area and need a job. I wanted to see if I couldn't find a better way to attract the kind of employee described above.

I remembered the advice of a psychology professor I had when I was attending the University of Mississippi years ago. His favorite expression was, "When you go fishing use the bait, not what you like, but that which attracts the fish."

With this expression in mind, I decided upon a completely new and indirect approach.

I was doing some special work at the time in recruiting for a large insurance company and this gave me a good opportunity to use this new approach. I began asking myself what it was that these people I wanted were looking for. What is it that would attract them?

They were certainly not looking for jobs. Not only did they have jobs but they loved their jobs. But I felt sure that while they were not at the time interested in changing their jobs, they *were* interested in changing and improving themselves. While these people were not particularly trying to *find* a better job, they were definitely concerned with preparing themselves to *do* a better job. The kind of person I was after realized full well that in order to build a future he must first start with building himself.

OPPORTUNITY FOR SELF-IMPROVEMENT THE ANSWER

The answer to my question finally became very clear to me. Since the type of person I was desirous of recruiting was interested in self-improvement more than anything else, if I wanted to locate and attract this person, I must offer him opportunity for self-improvement.

I explained my plan to the insurance company which I was representing in the recruiting activities. The company agreed to go along with me one hundred percent.

I began running display ads in the local newspaper, advertising a school to be held free of charge. It was labeled as a PERSONAL DEVELOPMENT COURSE. The ad carried the following heading:

HAVE YOU THE COURAGE TO ASK YOURSELF THESE IMPORTANT QUESTIONS?

"Are you a creature of circumstances or a creator of circumstances? Do you happen to things or do things happen to you?

"Do you have definite goals in life? Obstacles are those things we see when we take our eyes from our goals.

"Can you stand on your feet courageously, think clearly and express yourself in an articulate manner?"

When people answered the ad, I explained that there was no catch. There was no subterfuge or obligation of any sort. They were told that we were putting on this school for our own employees and that as a community service we were permitting members of the public, who truly were interested, to attend without charge. We further explained that the school was of equal quality and of the same type as those being put on elsewhere for a large fee.

I held these schools from 2:00 to 5:00 and from 7:00 to 10:00 for a week. In some places I held them for two weeks. Twenty were permitted to attend each class, making a total of forty. In every instance, I had more applications than I could possibly accommodate. More important than this, is the fact that those who answered the ad were alert, ambitious and eager to improve themselves.

I insisted that at least a third of each class be made up of present employees of the insurance company, preferably salesmen. This was for several reasons.

In the first place, we had represented that the school was being put on for the benefit of these employees and, of course, this had to be a truthful statement.

In the second place, the employees of the insurance company who wanted to take the course, by their mere desire to improve themselves proved that they were ambitious, dedicated to their work, enthusiastic, and of a caliber I needed in my recruiting program. These qualities are contagious and persuasive.

The third reason I wanted a large percentage of the class to be employees of the insurance company was that I knew that if they were going to attend, they would influence some of their friends in other lines of endeavor to attend also.

TRANSITION TO COMPANY

During the first few days of the school, nothing was ever mentioned about my company. However, after we had covered the subjects advertised, I explained that I was going to take many of the academic principles we had learned and apply them to a sales presentation. I explained that the reason I was going to use my service in the presentation was that I understood it best and could most easily apply it to the principles we had learned.

At this point, I went into a thorough and dynamic program of training salesmen to sell my service. The keynote of the training was that to be successful in this field, a salesman had to be both knowledgeable and dedicated. As a result, I stressed both the sales techniques and the great opportunity for service in my field of selling. This gave me an opportunity to sell my profession to a captive group who would listen attentively after I had gained their confidence. Never once in a dozen or more schools did I find this method offensive to anyone who attended the school.

I explained that we all had insurance on our lives, our homes, and our cars. Why shouldn't we have insurance on our incomes? I suggested that they master the presentation and learn all they could about our profession so that in the event they lost their present job, they could feel secure in a guaranteed income for themselves and their families. I convinced them that regardless of age or geography, they would be secure. They could follow the climate or go anywhere in the United States where there are people and immediately have a professional income.

TRIAL BASIS

The ambitious students buy this idea immediately. I am then ready for my next step. I convinced some that they could work on a part-time basis for a while just to prove that they could fall back on this type of work in the event of an emergency. These men already have the qualities that make for success in any field and are almost without exception successful.

I don't have to spell out the rest. Many of these people who were willing to go into insurance on a part-time basis quickly realized that by using the methods they just learned, they could earn more just working part time than they were earning at their present jobs. Also, they realized that by devoting full time to selling, they could double or triple their present income.

Many companies frown on part-time employees, even on a trial or training basis. This method of indirect recruiting works wonderfully well even where the intermediate trial step is not employed.

This method is not restricted just to the sales field. A company desiring any type of employee can use it.

SELF-SCREENING

One of the greatest advantages of this indirect way of recruiting is that it is the greatest screening method ever devised. Wouldn't you like to feel that every person with whom you are discussing employment is in your presence because he is interested in improving *himself*? How tragically different this is from the usual pattern of employment.

In the first place, the very ad itself eliminates all who are not self-improvement minded. You offer nothing in your ad except opportunity for improvement. You find that from the very beginning you are dealing with very deserving and ambitious material.

RECRUITING—THE BIG SALE

When one has the opportunity to be with a person for a week or two he has a real opportunity to sell him on going to work for a certain company.

Can you conceive of more favorable circumstances under which to make a sale? This is the most important of all sales—

selling a man on bettering his chances for success by joining your company.

It is very strange that many people fail to see that recruiting is the *"big sale"* in any business and that if they are to be successful, they must employ the same methods used in any other sale. Recruiting cannot be approached in a catch-as-catch-can manner.

Many sales managers, who realize that it would be colossal insanity to offer a product or service without going through the various steps of a sale, will nevertheless seek to employ a person by merely running an ad and, when a possible recruit shows up, do little more than tell him briefly about his company and hand him an application blank.

No one would be foolish enough to attempt the sale of stocks, insurance, or real estate in this manner. And yet these same people don't seem to realize that recruiting a good man is the most important sale of all—the one that requires and justifies an even greater effort than the sale of a mere product or service.

EACH STEP A MINOR DECISION

One important fact must not be overlooked. Each step of the school is accepted by the students as a minor decision.

First, they learn the academic principles of salesmanship. Then, they are taught to apply these principles to the sale of my product or service. They make another minor decision when they decide to try out the presentation in the field. Then they become part-time salesman just to prove that they can have the security of a second method of acquiring an income. Finally, after seeing the great opportunity, they cannot resist the temptation of embracing it as a full-time profession. Thus, these minor decisions finally add up to a major decision—the decision to join our company.

People who are recruited through this method are enthusiastic, but best of all, it is self-generated enthusiasm which comes from performance. Once they have embraced the profession, they begin to love this type of service even more than their former jobs to which they felt so attached. These men do not grab the paper and look for want ads each day as is the case with so many people who were hired through want ads. Most of these never saw a want ad—in fact, they never sought a job—jobs always sought them.

JUST TRY IT

I strongly recommend this procedure to any company or individual desiring a high type of permanent personnel. I'm sure some will not feel favorable to the idea. All I can do is repeat a good old southern phrase. "If you ain't tried it, don't knock it."

The method is not expensive. Practically every town has many graduates of Sales Training Inc., Dale Carnegie and Toastmaster courses who are well qualified and eager to work with you. You do not need to have an outside sales consultant come in. By planning such a course and offering it to the public as a community service, you will not only secure some of the finest permanent employees ever to enter your business, but you will also make many friends for your company and build a priceless public image.

CHAPTER 14

THE ANATOMY OF PERSUASION

While this book is not directed exclusively to any restricted business, industry or profession, there is one principle we should always keep in mind.

Whether a person is a doctor, lawyer, merchant, chief; whether he is a priest, prophet, pawn-broker or peanut vendor; everyone is in the sales field—in the business of persuasion. The doctor sells his patients, the lawyer sells his jury, the pastor sells his congregation, the lover sells his sweetheart, and yes, the peanut vendor sells you his peanuts.

This doesn't mean that we use the same methods. Our end results may not be the same, but everyone, without exception, stands in the market place today and mentally shouts, "Who will buy my wares?"

I'm sure you agree with me that the process of persuading people to think and act as we desire is the very essence of our existence. In fact it is the balance wheel that gives stability not only to our entire economic system, but to life itself.

The ability to persuade others to act in a predetermined manner is the sole ingredient that transforms products and ideas into service and service into income.

Remember that except for the fact that the world finally recognized persuasion as the only civilized method of living with our fellow man, we all would still be carrying around our club of prehistoric days. Even today, unless we learn the simple art of persuasion we shall find ourselves constantly in a state of disenchantment.

Furthermore, we know that the keystone to the arch of persuasion is knowledge of the component parts of a sale. Unless we understand all the ingredients of persuasion, the part played by each, their sequence and just how each relates and harmonizes with the other, we shall never be effective in the human engineering art of persuading our fellow man.

In this chapter we shall discuss the principal ingredients of the anatomy of persuasion. Regardless of what your endeavors in life may be, these principles apply in some measure to your activities. Maybe they apply a little stronger to some activities than to others, but we are all in the "people business" and as long as we deal with people we are handicapped unless we know how to persuade.

As we go from one step to the next, please try to relate the principles discussed to your particular everyday experiences. In this way you can realize the maximum benefits.

COMPONENT PARTS OF A SALE

I am very much impressed with the fact that one of the large typewriter companies will not let a service man go out on a service call until he can, while blindfolded, take a typewriter apart and put it back together again. I can't even change a ribbon with my glasses on.

Can we take our sales presentation apart and put it back together? Do we know what makes it work; how it is organized; the relationship of each part to the other; how the parts all harmonize and finally lead to a focal point, down to the magic point of action—the moment of truth—getting the signature where necessary?

I recently consulted the dictionary for the definition of anatomy. Anatomy means the component parts of any body. If we haven't already done so, let's dissect the sale and look at several of its parts.

THE CLOSE

Just as our heart is the mainspring of life we know that the CLOSE is the heart of our entire sales program. We know that everything we do or say in our presentation that is not related to the close should be thrown out. It is absolutely useless. There is no excuse for effort except for action and no excuse for action except for results.

If we motivate a person to think positively, that is fine, but it's only a preliminary step. Unless we can also motivate him to act positively our entire endeavor has been only an academic experience. Thought put into motion is power; thought remaining static is sterile and of no value. Sometimes it is very hard for an inexperienced person to realize this fully.

I had a grandfather who wore his Confederate uniform until the day he died. He had a next door neighbor by the name of Mr. Shimmel who did the same. Mr. Shimmel received monthly a little $18 pension check from the Government.

The first of each month Mr. Shimmel would make quite a ceremony of receiving that little check. One day my grandfather was down at the rural mail box when Mr. Shimmel ran his hand up in the box and smilingly said, "Come here, Emmet, I want to show you something."

As he opened the letter and exhibited the check he proudly said, "Do you see that signature on the bottom of that check? That's the signature of the President of the United States of America. He is an important man—about the most important man on this continent. And, Emmet, do you see the signature just below his? That's the signature of the Treasurer of the United States. He's an important man, too. He controls all the money in the country."

And then, as Mr. Shimmel drew himself up to his full height, he turned the check over and said, "Emmet do you see that little thin line on the back of this check? That's where I put MY signature. And you know something, Emmet, until I put my signature right there, as important as those two men may be, their signatures ain't worth a damn."

The reason I like that story is this: You can go out and educate your prospect, you can entertain him, you can wine and dine with him, but unless you are able to close, enjoyable as these things may be, they do not accomplish anything—you have not rendered a service.

THE CLOSE—THE FOCAL POINT OF ACTION

Any intelligent approach to a presentation must start out with the major premise that the sole purpose of any presentation is directed to causing a person to act. Everything we say or do, like an inverted cone, leads to a final focal point—where rests at *one spot* the impact of our entire interview. We call this the focal point of action. Anything contained in our presentation that does not lead to this one focal point is distracting and should be thrown out of the presentation. It ruins the symmetry of the cone.

Approach each prospect committed to this principle and you will find that your energies are more productive. The "art of persuasion" may be the key to a sale, but only bringing your prospect to the magic focal point of action unlocks the door. Unless you learn how to organize your entire efforts into one impact, to concentrate your entire approach into one final blow and bring it with force to the point of the inverted cone, you are in reality not selling at all. You belong to that time-consuming group known as commercial visitors.

And how do we organize our presentation in such a way that we can be sure we lead our prospect directly to this vulnerable spot—this focal point of action? How do we keep from dissipating our energies to no avail—ending up the victim of a confused and useless interview?

We accomplish this by starting out early in our presentation to feel our prospect's buying pulse and to watch for a *CLOSING*

SIGNAL. Whenever we do receive that buying signal, we know then that our interview has reached that focal point of action and we are ready for the close.

TRIAL CLOSES

And what are the tools we use constantly to test for this buying signal? The tools used are known as *Trial Closes.*

A trial close is just what the name signifies. It is only a trial. We lose nothing nor are we discouraged if we do not get the closing signal. We simply continue, but never, never take our finger from our prospect's buying pulse.

To trial close, simply offer an advantage or benefit or reason for buying and then ask for a minor decision. If the minor decision does not bring forth the closing signal, suggest more reasons for buying, constantly building up more benefits, and then feel his pulse again for the buying signal. This is a very simple process once we have learned it. We can continue this method with as many trial closes as are required, but remember—always give additional reasons for buying before each new trial close.

Start out your trial closes conscious of the fact that everyone, without exception, has at least one responsive note—one vulnerable spot that *can* be reached. Your job is to find, by testing, just what is your prospect's responsive note—his vulnerable spot. If you proceed carefully, and if you study your prospect thoroughly, you are bound to find it in one of the five great motivating factors that cause us to act. These are *Pride, Profit, Need, Love and Fear.*

These five motivating factors were treated in more detail in Chapter 5 of this book.

BUYING SIGNAL IN THE FORM OF AN OBJECTION

Also remember this: Very, very seldom is our buying signal a direct signal—a *yes* signal. It is in most cases an indirect signal—a closing signal sometimes even in the form of an *objection.* Instead of being upset by an objection, you should greet it cheerfully and enthusiastically.

An objection, to the human engineer, is only a challenge. He realizes that the act of persuasion does not begin until a person has voiced an objection.

Here, briefly, is a four point magic formula which the human engineer uses in meeting objections:

First, he acts delighted.

"I'm glad you brought that up."

"That's a good point."

Second, he repeats the objection in the form of a question, which takes the sting out of the word "objection" and in fact calls for an answer.

"The question in your mind is whether you feel this machine will do the job, isn't it?"

Third, he gets the commitment that this is the only question.

"Except for this one question you would go along with the program, wouldn't you? There is no other question in your mind, is there?"

Finally, the human engineer, where possible, concentrates on the one point brought up in the objection, elaborating on its favorable aspects.

"I'm glad to see that this is an important point with you because this is the best phase of our service—in fact, the phase of which we are most proud."

If this is impossible then he points out some other phase of the product or service which is more important.

"This is true, as you say, but have you considered the important economy aspect? No other similar product can compete with it in this regard."

DELAY ANSWERING OBJECTIONS WHERE POSSIBLE

While you should never give the impression that you are avoiding an objection, yet, whenever possible, as was said earlier in this book, you should postpone answering any objection until you have covered all five motivating factors with trial closes.

One of these things will usually happen: You will cover the point in your presentation, or it will be forgotten if the objection was unreal, or the prospects will ignore it in their enthusiasm for some other aspect of the presentation which is more important to them.

"I'm certainly glad you brought that up, Mr. Jones. I know exactly how you feel, and I will cover that later, if you don't mind."

If, however, you feel that the objection should be answered at the time it is given, then use the four-step magic formula for answering objections.

MUSTS IN USING TRIAL CLOSES

In presenting trial closes by all means observe these two important rules:

First, do not forget the grandeur and the greatness of simplicity. A confused mind hardens just as cement does. As we stress in Chapter 3, people are never persuaded by what we say, but only by what they understand. Think ahead of them, but by all means don't GET ahead of them. Pause often and ask if you are making yourself clear. If your presentation could not be understood by an eighth grader, the chances are more than likely that your presentation is over your prospect's head. You must be conscious of this during every minute of your presentation.

Second, and of utmost importance, is this warning: *Don't do all of the talking!* Each trial close is designed to get an expression from your prospect and start him talking. Give him every opportunity to do so. Every form of true communication requires two parties. Unless your prospect is given time to express himself, even if it is to voice an objection, you will have no indication of what he is thinking. You have no way of knowing whether you have touched his responsive note or not.

DON'T BUY IT BACK

I've been out with salesmen and watched them make a beautiful sale, only to see them keep on talking until they "bought it back." They talked so much themselves that they didn't take time to recognize the buying signal.

Occasionally when I am giving a human engineering seminar and want to be sure that those attending will remember this point, I tell the story of Bill and Joe.

Bill and Joe were out mountain climbing. Joe slipped and fell down into a little crevice. In addition to his pain he was afraid he would freeze to death. He began screaming for help.

Bill dropped him a rope and said, "Hold on to the rope, Joe, and I'll get you out."

Joe yelled back and said, "I can't, my arms are broken."

"Tie the rope around your waist," continued Bill.

"I can't," said Joe, "my back is broken."

Whereupon Bill urged him, "Joe don't worry, I'll get you out. Now listen, take hold of the rope with your teeth and hold on. I'll put you up."

So Joe did and Bill began the tedious task of slowly pulling Joe up. Finally, as beads of perspiration were breaking out on Bill and he had Joe within a few feet of the top, he smiled joyously and said, "We made it, didn't we Joe?"

Joe, as he sank out of sight, was heard to say, "Yeeeeeeeehh."

How many times have we all persuaded a person completely; yet, had the sale within our very grasp and then "bought it back" by talking too much? Yes, we open our mouths and lose it.

NOTHING MATTERS IF YOU CAN'T CLOSE

Not long ago I was holding a human engineer seminar for a large insurance company on the West Coast.

The appearance of a certain young salesman would indicate that he had everything. He had good looks, personality; he could communicate and even motivate. The only thing wrong was that he didn't close any sales.

So disturbed and confused was I about his lack of production that I decided to call on a few of the families he had approached.

When I called on the first family, the lady of the house said, "Is that young fellow in your company? He is one of the nicest young men we have ever had in our home. We kept him here the other night almost until midnight. I even cut a pie we were saving for the next day and all of us had pie and coffee."

I inquired carefully, "Did you sign an application for a policy?"

"No, no," was the reply, "I didn't buy anything but I was impressed by his personality."

I met with the same experience on my next call.

"I paid that young man the highest compliment I ever paid anyone in my home," the lady enthusiastically said. "I even stopped my son from studying to come in and listen to him. And when he left, I told my son that he had just seen the kind of person I wanted him to be when he grew up."

Again I asked, "Did he give you an opportunity to sign an application for protection?"

I received practically the same discouraging answer, "No, we didn't discuss business very much, but we were so impressed with him. You certainly have a valuable employee in that boy."

This fellow was good to everyone except his family. Everyone loved him except his creditors. This boy was not out selling. He was only a *commercial visitor out protecting his ego from the emotional trauma of a refusal. He wouldn't risk failure.*

After much deliberation and battling with my conscience, I finally recommended to his superiors that unless they wanted to establish a retirement home for attractive young men in their twenties, they would do the boy and themselves a favor by taking him off a drawing account, which he dearly loved, and letting him take his attractions elsewhere.

Never forget that the ability to close, the power to move a person to action, is the very heart of the anatomy of persuasion.

PROSPECTING

Just as the close is the very heart of our presentation in considering the anatomy of a sale, we know that PROSPECTING constitutes the lungs from which we receive the very breath of life.

I say without fear of contradiction that the great mortality rate among salesmen is due more to poor prospecting than to any other cause. I've known salesmen who claimed to be good closers; they claimed they were good in all fields of persuasion but they just didn't seem to expose themselves enough to be productive. They didn't seem to realize that you must circulate if you expect to percolate—you must make contacts if you expect to make contracts.

Recently one of the largest sales organizations in America employed a business analysis firm to contact over a thousand former "commission salesmen" in different parts of our country and find out why they had not remained in the sales field.

Over 80 percent reported it was because they had not been able to make enough presentations. Many boasted of a very high closing rate. This meant nothing to them, however, if they didn't have a place to go and expose this talent.

What would you think of a drug store, clothing store, or hardware store that opened for business and had no inventory on its shelves? A salesman's good current prospect cards are his inventory. Without them he is both hopeless and helpless. He is not even in business.

We have heard for many years the old expression, "A merchant can't sell from an empty cart." And yet, I know salesmen today who try. Furthermore, 80 percent of one thousand ex-salesmen tried, and, of course, failed.

All my life I have heard it said, *"Your prospects for success* in any field of selling depend almost entirely on the *success of your prospecting."* If a person can realize *this* early in his selling career and furthermore realize that there are no "shortcuts" in prospecting, his chances for success in the sales field are greatly increased.

WHERE DO I GET MY PROSPECTS?

Whenever a young salesman asks me where he is to get his

prospects I like to tell him the story of the little town back in olden days that was "rat infested."

The people became panicky. They were afraid the rats might cause the "bubonic plague."

Finally a man appeared in the town one day who claimed to be a "rat expert." So the city elders got in touch with him and he entered into a contract with them to kill all of the rats.

They paid him and he was to start at daylight the next day. Sure enough, he arrived early the next morning in the city square with a big stump and cleaver and proclaimed loudly, "Now bring on your rats."

I try to explain to young salesmen that if we didn't need prospects we would not need nearly as many salesmen. If you could put me in front of prospects all day who had been screened and who would listen to me with an open mind, I could do the job of fifty salesmen, and I am sure others could do this also.

The more professional our endeavors are, the more time we should spend in preliminary work. A lawyer spends ten hours preparing a law suit for each hour he spends trying the suit in court. An architect spends fifteen to twenty hours making his drawings for each hour he spends showing his renderings. A teacher, professor, speaker, pastor all spend much preliminary time in preparation.

Why should a salesman feel it is at all out of line for him to spend two or three hours prospecting for each hour he spends making a presentation in the presence of a prospect? Accept this fact early in your career: There is no substitute—there is no short cut in the field of prospecting.

The human engineer who has chosen selling as his profession realizes fully that any time that he is not facing a prospect or prospecting to make such an interview possible, he is unemployed.

WHY IS PROSPECTING NEGLECTED?

If you can agree with me at this point that prospecting is the most important single step in successful selling—then let's analyze for a moment the reasons prospecting is so sadly neglected today.

First, I believe it is because only a few salesmen realize that the nature of our industry is such that time and effort are *required* in order to secure prospects. Time-consuming as it may be, it is of such great importance that it justifies all the time necessary.

If a salesman will only realize the fact that there *must* be this ratio mentioned above, and if he is willing to adjust his schedule and work habits to conform to this fact, then he will find that selling offers one of the greatest opportunities in our entire economic society.

But if he is unwilling to do this; if he tries to find an easier way; if he tries to substitute personality for performance; pull for hard work; luck for work habits—then he will go the way of the 80 percent who tried but couldn't find a substitute either.

Yes, I repeat—the first reason many men neglect putting proper emphasis upon prospecting is that they don't realize that prospecting is the breath of life of all selling—the ultimate, the acme of our sales existence.

Another reason that many salesmen neglect proper prospecting is too obvious to need elaboration. Regrettably they suffer from that human malady that seems to permeate many businesses today. It is *Laziness.*

No cure has yet been found for this, but so contagious is the disease that it is strongly recommended the patient be quarantined from other salesmen—permanently.

METHODS OF PROSPECTING

And now that, hopefully, you agree with me on the importance of prospecting, let's look at the *methods* of prospecting.

Inasmuch as a salesman gets 85 to 90 percent of all his prospects from three methods of prospecting, it seems best to confine our treatment to these three methods. They are *radiation*, *referral*, and *survey*. Survey is also known as canvassing or P.D.C. (which means Personal Direct Contact).

LEADS THROUGH RADIATION

First, let's consider RADIATION. Leads through radiation means friends, relatives, the butcher, the baker, the man running the gas station or the corner store, your lodge brother, your neighbor across the street—people with whom you associate in both a business and a social way.

Some salesmen hesitate to contact this group for fear they might feel he is taking advantage of friendship or business connections. This is a most unfortunate attitude and springs either from the fact that the salesman himself is not completely sold on his product or service or from the fact that the salesman uses the wrong approach.

If your relatives or close friends are not thoroughly acquainted with your service, this suggested approach might be of great help to you:

"John, I'm engaged in a most interesting line of work. I'd like to get your ideas about it. I want you to listen to my presentation—not as a prospect, but as a critic."

Believe me, he will listen and furthermore since he doesn't feel under the pressure of making a decision, he will listen with an open mind. This method is no subterfuge—you can use it and be mentally honest. You *do* want his opinion.

If you do a good job, the chances are just as good that he will want to buy your product as they would have been if you had approached him solely for the purpose of selling him. The fact is, your chances are better and for very obvious reasons.

Does your grocer feel embarrassed to talk with you about his groceries? Does your milkman hesitate to discuss his product? Does your butcher, baker, gas attendant fail to discuss his services with you?

Be careful, however, when you approach a person in this category that you sell *only* the interview—don't discuss your product or service. If you confine your efforts solely to selling the interview, you will be amazed to find that you will not receive a refusal. If he states that he cannot buy your product, assure him that this is not the primary reason for your presentation. If he states that he will be glad to listen to you but that you would be wasting your time, assure him that it will not be a waste of time because you will profit from his opinion. On the original approach, do not discuss or even think beyond the interview. When a salesman has finally learned to divorce the sale of the interview from the sale of his product or service, he will find that his prospect file will begin to grow.

Any salesman who does not take advantage of this valuable group of prospects, which he can secure from RADIATION, has foolishly deprived himself of one of the primary sources of good leads. Don't unnecessarily cut down your opportunity for success by ignoring this group.

LEADS THROUGH REFERRALS

Now for REFERRALS I'd almost rather miss a sale than make one and fail to secure several good referred prospects. The thoroughness with which I have convinced my customer in making the sale can, in most cases, be measured by his willingness and even eagerness to give me referrals.

Yes, each good sale automatically generates several good prospects. These leads are of particular value because they are so approachable. "Your friends, Mr. And Mrs. Thomas, asked me to drop by and visit with you."

If at the close of a sale a person gives me a name but asks that I do not reveal the source of the reference, I do not consider it a referral and in fact give it very little consideration. If I have properly sold my product or my service, my customer is desirous of having his friends receive these same advantages without any reservations—otherwise it is not a solid sale. I have made an extensive study of this situation. These studies reveal conclusively what we could have surmised even without research:

The customers who enthusiastically give me referrals without reservation have a delinquency rate in payments which is practically nil.

Those who give referrals but ask that I do not reveal the source have a much higher delinquency rate.

The highest delinquency rate of all belongs to those who hesitate to give any referrals at all.

Willie Hoppe was the greatest billiard player of his generation. His repeated tournament wins were due to the fact that so delicate was his touch that he could make a billiard ball stop at a position which "set up" and made his next shot easy.

We can apply the same principle to sales. Any sale that does not lead to or make the next sale easier is lacking in some respect.

I suggest strongly that you never neglect this secondary sale which can bring you dividends far beyond your wildest imagination, *provided* you give it the importance it deserves. I repeat, "You will find this group of leads the most approachable of all."

LEADS THROUGH CANVASSING

To be most effective, leads must be produced in *volume*, produced economically, and, perhaps of greatest importance, in a concentrated area. I say "in a concentrated area" because the "golden hours of presentation"—the hours in the presence of a prospect—are so few and priceless that you can't afford to dissipate this precious time driving from one part of the city to another seeking an opportunity to make a presentation.

This brings us to the third and only certain way of acquiring leads in abundance, inexpensively, and in concentration. I refer, of course, to SURVEY, CANVASSING or P.D.C. (Personal Direct Contact). It matters little what you call it as long as you DO IT!

If you actually make up your mind that you are going to learn the proper way to survey, it can actually become fun. Then, pursued regularly and on a schedule, it will keep you optimistic and you'll always have a place to go. Remember, any time you don't have a place to go, you're unemployed—you're out of a job.

Yes, survey—done properly—can be enjoyable. If you learn to relax and look for friendly, courteous people—that's just what you'll find. But if you expect to find cold unfriendly people, you'll not be disappointed.

It is YOU and YOU ALONE who determines the reception you will get at the home or office door. We've all been taught from childhood that the *world is a looking glass and gives back to every person a reflection of his own attitude.* I repeat this important principle throughout this book.

It might all be summed up in one sentence: *Whether you think people are friendly or whether you think people are unfriendly, you're right.*

Now for a few suggestions to make your survey most effective.

Be casual, relaxed, and never give the impression that you are in a hurry. If you are tense and nervous, your prospect will not open up. He also will be tense. Many salesmen attempt to get information quickly, with as few words as possible, and bound away before a conversation is begun.

If you become a discipline of this *Hit and Run* group, I guarantee you will never learn to enjoy surveying and furthermore, I assure you that you will not receive maximum benefits. Certainly I don't advocate that you reveal anything about the merits of your product or service while surveying or that you become encumbered in a long conversation. But there is a happy medium which you should eventually develop.

Second, when you survey, you are not looking for people who are interested in your product or service, but only for people who will give you an appointment so that you can make your presentation. Accept the fact that you will not find people on your survey who are interested in buying your product. If such people existed they would already have come to your company and bought. You are only looking for people who will listen. Now *you* listen carefully and consider this statement which all successful surveyors realize is true: *It is easier to sell to a person who is not interested than to find a person who is interested.* If he gives you an interview it is up to you to interest him.

DON'T SELL ON YOUR SURVEY

The most important thing in your survey is to have your

prospect keep an open mind. Nothing causes a person to shut his mind quicker and "clam up" than to feel that he is faced with a DECISION. That's why we don't want our prospect even to consider the advantages or disadvantages of our product or service on the survey—just the advantages of having valuable information.

I have found one point in my survey very important. If you are willing to go out and use it constantly, you will eventually agree with me wholeheartedly regarding its importance.

If I am making a survey in a residential area to determine the need for my product or service, after knocking on the door or pressing the bell, I step back well away from the door. I have a large clip-board and have my pen poised for writing. When the party comes to the door, she sees that she is not faced with the decision of whether to let me in or not. Therefore she is not tense but relaxed.

Now comes the important part. It works like magic. I simply smile and say casually and jovially, "Good morning. I wonder if you can help me with a little information."

Then hesitate and wait for an answer. You'll spoil it all if you act in a hurry or fail to wait for an answer.

I can tell you what the answer will be nine times out of ten. It will be one of the following:

"Well, I hope so," or

"Perhaps I can," or

"What seems to be the trouble?"

Now why do you receive such answers in a friendly tone? I'll tell you why.

BREAKING DOWN PERSONAL BARRIERS

One of the basic principles of human engineering is this: The method of breaking down personal barriers is to do one of three things: tell a secret, make a confession, or, MOST IMPORTANT OF ALL—ask a favor.

It's a natural human trait that people enjoy being asked to do a favor—they enjoy even more *doing* it.

If you have not found surveying a pleasure up to this point, try what I have suggested. It is almost miraculous to note the different response you will receive during the survey interview, simply by putting the prospect in the role of being helpful.

This same principle applies to office calls, telephone calls and to all means of communication.

Have you ever known of a failure in the sales field by a person who put emphasis on all three methods of prospecting? I am sure you haven't. Furthermore, I doubt if you have ever known of a success in the sales field by one who neglects habitual and constant prospecting.

Yes, prospecting is like shaving. Unless you do it every day, you'll soon be a BUM.

I hope you will read this chapter many times. Practice the three methods of prospecting—especially the survey. The principles are useless unless followed religiously.

I emphasize once more the theme of good prospecting. Never forget it—it can mean the extra margin that will elevate you to a new plateau of professional selling.

Your prospect for success in any field of selling depends almost entirely on the success of your prospecting.

THE PRESENTATION

Just as our bone structure gives form and substance to our body, our presentation is the bone structure of our entire sales program.

I made a hobby of collecting presentations at one time. I possessed the one which was used around the turn of the century. It was simply "Pose the problem, Offer the solution and Ask for action."

Then in the twenties we had the very popular one labeled AIDA. This was the "Attention, Interest, Desire, and Action Presentation."

Finally in the late twenties and early thirties we had the Borden and Bussy and the Dale Carnegie version, known as the

"Ho-hum, Why bring that up, For instance, So what" formula.

They are all good if we use them correctly. However, regardless of what presentation we use, we must do three things in order to make any of them effective:

We must get together with our prospect PHYSICALLY so that we can talk with him.

We must get together with him MENTALLY so that he will listen.

And finally, we must harmonize with him EMOTIONALLY so that he will act.

This formula is the essence of simplicity but it has the homely virtue of working.

One thing we must realize from the very beginning. We do not have an interview with our prospect until we are with him both physically and mentally.

APPROACH AND PRESENTATION

For the sake of clarity, let's divide our presentation into two parts. The first is the APPROACH and the second is the actual PRESENTATION itself.

For even further simplicity we can consider the APPROACH as divided into two parts. First, we have GETTING THE INTERVIEW and second, the NEUTRALIZATION PERIOD, also known as the WARMING-UP PERIOD.

These various steps in making a sale may at first seem a little confusing. However, if we analyze them carefully and study them thoroughly, we can see that in reality they are clear, logical, and follow each other in natural sequence.

Before considering each step carefully, let's repeat them once again.

First, we "get with our prospect physically" by gaining the interview.

Second, we "get with him mentally" through the neutralization or warming up period.

Third and finally, we "harmonize with him emotionally"

through the procedure in the actual presentation.

If these three steps are taken carefully, then our prospect is ready to buy. We are prepared for completing the contract or finalizing the sale, which is the subject of the CLOSE, covered earlier in this chapter.

IMPORTANCE OF INTERVIEW AND NEUTRALIZATION

Too little importance is usually placed on the first two steps of the sale, that is, gaining the interview and the neutralization period. Experienced salesmen all agree that when we have gained the interview and have properly opened the mind of our prospect after the warming up period, 60 percent of the sale is accomplished. This means that 60 percent of the work contributing to success is done before we even begin our actual presentation.

Now since this is true, I'm sure you will agree with me that getting into the home or office and creating a climate conducive to success is of tremendous importance.

GAINING THE INTERVIEW

Let's first consider getting into the home or office—that is, getting the interview. I'm sure you will not forget this major premise, this undisputed fact: "The hardest door you will ever find to open is your own—the door you must open to go out and call on people."

The average person is a genius in creating reasons, at the last minute, why he should not go out and make calls.

And so our task of entering through doors to make adequate presentations is partially solved when we have developed the self-discipline necessary to open our own door each day or night, as the case may be, and enthusiastically go out and call on people.

Even after we are out, a door often assumes the role of a monster baring its teeth and daring us to knock. This is true—it happens to us all. It's nothing to be ashamed of.

The fact is—we don't want to remove the butterflies from your stomach. We only want to teach them to fly in formation. Courage isn't overcoming fear—it's standing your ground in spite of it.

You might say, "O.K., it's nice to have your platitudes and sterile clichés but HOW do I cope with fear? Don't pose a problem without offering a solution."

That's a position well taken, but in this case we can say the solution is certain—the answer is definite. It is found in a law as old as time itself.

Newton described the principle so clearly that it has been given his name. We speak of it as Newton's Second Law:

"For every force there must be an equal and opposite force."

It is only natural that fear and apprehension exert a force upon us when we approach the door, not knowing what is behind it. The force pushes us back, making it difficult to proceed.

Unless we have within ourselves certain forces such as enthusiasm, determination and dedication, to overcome the opposing force, we cannot move forward. We are held immobile or are pushed backward.

And so the frame of mind of the salesman as he approaches the door is the all-important factor at this point. If he waits until he reaches the office or home before getting into the proper attitude, he is helpless.

THE HUMAN ENGINEER

The human engineer starts preparing himself to approach the prospect's door as soon as he wakes up in the morning. It is a great day and life is full of magic for the very good reason that he is determined to go out and make it so. He is proud of his profession—he believes in what he is doing. When asked what he does for a living, he doesn't dig his toe, twist a button and evade the question. He is proud to say, "I am a salesman."

SERVICE SIGN VS. DOLLAR SIGN

When the salesman approaches the door he should approach

it in a problem-solving attitude. Unless he sees the SERVICE sign on the door rather than the dollar sign, he is licked before he starts.

Sometimes I imagine that my prospect's office or house is on fire—yes, being burned down by the fires of inflation which I can put out by causing him to buy my product at today's prices. With that feeling of urgency, I can't be refused entrance.

I approach as a guest who expects to be invited in so I can share my valuable ideas. So expectant do I feel, that almost unconsciously, my prospect conforms to my expectancy.

Now this is important: After introducing yourself and stating your company's name, immediately and enthusiastically say, "May I come in?" If this is done quickly, without hesitancy, you will be amazed how many times you will be invited in without any question.

If a question is asked you regarding your mission, answer it briefly and again say enthusiastically, "May I be your guest a few minutes to explain it to you?"

If a further question is put to you, don't evade it—answer it directly in as few words as possible and *again* say "May I step in and briefly tell you about it?"

The point is that if you counter each question politely with a request to be permitted to come in, any long conversation at the office or home door can be avoided.

KEYNOTE IS ENTHUSIASM

Above all else, *act enthusiastic*. It's the most engaging and disarming attitude you can assume.

If you desire to talk with both the husband and wife and they are both home, immediately say, "Oh, I'm so glad I found you both here." Step back so the door can be opened.

If you find a man at his office, take the same enthusiastic attitude, letting him know how delighted you are that you found him in. Any person is complimented if you are genuinely enthusiastic about seeing him.

If you still find it difficult to gain entrance, say something such as this: "Mr. Jones, you are sole judge of whether my service interests you or not. But I do have some information you will appreciate having."

Then again quickly follow with, "May I come in, so I can explain it to you briefly?"

If your prospect resists further or insists that you explain your mission on the threshold, politely excuse yourself with, "Maybe some other time when you are not busy, I'm sorry you don't have the time because you would have thanked me."

I repeat, never tell your mission on the doorstep of a home or at an office door. Doorsteps and thresholds were meant only as a means by which to enter a building or room—never as a platform or podium from which to make your presentation.

If you follow these suggestions implicitly, you will find yourself in most cases within the office or home.

Once having entered, you have crossed the first bridge. You are with your prospect physically.

NEUTRALIZATION OR WARMING UP PERIOD

Now you must get together with your prospect mentally by means of the neutralization or warming up period. If you enjoy people, you should have no trouble with the warming up period.

Remember this always—a man's house or his office is his castle and he should be treated as king at all times. Being assumptuous is fine—assume that he will accept your service. But don't be presumptuous—this is fatal.

Control the situation and direct the conversation, but don't dominate the premises. If you act as a guest, eager to solve a problem and be of service, you will find that you will be treated as a guest and will be given a hearing with an open mind.

As we emphasized earlier, we would not dive into water without first testing the temperature and depth. It would be equally foolish to dive into your presentation before you had tested your prospects through a few pleasantries and created a friendly atmosphere. On the other hand, you are there on an important matter. Get down to business as soon as possible.

Try to be as observant as possible. If your prospects have trophies, ask about them. If they were not proud of them, they would not be displaying them.

If they have many family pictures around, you may be fairly certain that you can get a response by discussing their children. The first few seconds after you enter the office or house must be "played by ear."

If you will take the trouble to make a little pre-call preparation and learn a few facts about your prospects, the extra effort will pay off handsomely during the warming up period. On referrals especially, always try to arm yourself with all the personal knowledge you can assemble.

RELEASE ANY PRESSURE

I have found that the best way to complete a neutralization or warming up period and make sure that I am with my prospect mentally as well as physically, is to make my prospect feel from the very beginning that he has a way out—that he can gracefully say "NO" should he be faced with a decision.

I have found this helpful: "Mr. and Mrs. Jones, you'll be sole judge of whether or not this fits into your program. Even if it does, there is no reason why you should feel compelled to accept our service, if you prefer to secure it elsewhere. My job primarily is to see that you understand our program."

This also has been effective: "Mr. and Mrs. Jones, if I should unintentionally say anything to influence you, please caution me. Any decision you make must be your own. I only want to be sure you receive *all* the facts so that you can make an intelligent decision."

It is important that you get with your prospect mentally. Perhaps the most basic of all sales principles is that you must *open* the mind to *close* the sale.

It is equally important, however, that once you have opened

his mind, you proceed with the PRESENTATION without delay.

Our first two steps are now behind us. We are with our prospect both physically and mentally. Now the ultimate goal of our PRESENTATION is to harmonize with him emotionally and prepare him for execution of the contract.

THE ACTUAL PRESENTATION

At this point, the curtain is about to rise on the first act in our little drama which we call the PRESENTATION. The act is divided into four scenes, each entirely separate, and each with a specific purpose that must be accomplished if our drama is to be a success. These were only mentioned briefly in the early part of this book.

In the first scene, we must get our prospect's *attention*. To do this we must make ourselves *understood*.

In the second scene, we must create *interest* in our service. To do this we must make our prospects *like us*.

In the third scene, we must produce overwhelming *conviction and desire*. To do this, we must make our prospects *believe* us.

In the fourth and final scene, we must create an impulse to *act*. We must make the prospect WANT what we have to offer. To do this, we must make our prospects *trust us*.

When these four steps have been taken, we are finally ready for the close which we have already covered. These four steps must be in logical sequence—never out of order—and each must be pursued with equal determination.

Now let's expand on these four scenes.

ATTENTION THROUGH UNDERSTANDING US

Our first challenge is to be sure that we get the ATTENTION of our prospect. We can do this only if we are completely understood. Let's remember that while our product or service is thoroughly understood by us, it is new to our prospect. Our presentation will not even get off of the ground unless our initial approach to our prospect is simple, clear and articulate.

When we first approach our prospect we must remember that we are competing for his attention. He already has other things on his mind. We must make our approach so clear, interesting and understandable that these other matters are pushed into the background. Unless we can do this we will not get his attention.

INTEREST THROUGH LIKING US

Our second task, as we have stated, is to arouse *Interest* in our product or service. To do this, our story must be told with *Romance, Drama,* and most important of all—with *Enthusiasm.* ENTHUSIASM—one of the greatest moving forces on earth! Nothing great in life can be accomplished without it. Without it we cannot succeed—with it we cannot fail. Everyone LIKES and enjoys being around an enthusiastic person.

How can we expect anyone to be enthusiastic or even interested in our product or service unless we ourselves are enthusiastic? We will never find a method of creating INTEREST in our product or service to equal being interested and enthusiastic about it ourselves.

DESIRE THROUGH BELIEVING US

And now that we have aroused interest, we shift to the third scene of our drama. We must *convince* our prospects and create a DESIRE. We must make them *believe us.* Yes, we must prove our case. We must convert the prospect to our way of thinking.

Remember—nothing destroys confidence more quickly than generalities and statements we cannot prove. People are not convinced by claims. They are persuaded only by *Proof, Evidence, Facts.*

If you doubt this, ask any judge or jury. In this case, it is your prospects who are the jury—it is *they* who will give the verdict.

To convince, be specific, use testimonials, offer "quotes." Show written guarantees, use examples and analogies freely and above all, use *comparisons.*

Yes, the best yardstick we can use to test the value of any product or service is the yardstick of comparison. Comparisons make up the very heart of our presentation.

Compare the advantages of your product or service with the disadvantages of being without it. Compare prices, if price is a factor. Compare the advantages of acting now with the dangers of waiting.

Don't neglect true stories that you can preface with: "We have found," "People tell us," "This happened recently."

ACTION THROUGH TRUSTING US

And finally we come to the fourth scene in our drama. We first gained our prospect's attention by making him understand us; then we gained his interest by being enthusiastic and making him like us; next, we created a desire on his part by giving proof, evidence, facts, and making him believe us.

Now we must move our prospect to action by making him trust us. This is the supreme test of human engineering. You earn this right to be trusted only by the manner in which you deal with your prospect.

If you truly have your prospect's interest at heart, if you are more interested in solving his problem than in your personal gain, it will be apparent to him. Sincerity cannot be faked.

Remember that your prospect, when he is about to act, wants assurance that he is doing the right thing. Only a person he can trust is capable of giving this assurance.

If we have made ourselves understood, liked, believed and finally trusted, then we can be sure that we have gained attention, interest and desire, and that our prospect is prepared to act. Then we can say that the curtain falls on a very successful four-scene drama called *The Presentation*.

START USING THESE PRINCIPLES NOW

This chapter, *The Anatomy of Persuasion,* is by far the longest chapter in this book. It goes into some of the aspects of persuasion in detail and for emphasis repeats others mentioned earlier in this book. This is because of the importance of these principles. Remember that we all are engaged in selling and can profit by sales principles and procedures. Absolutely no one is exempt from the need of this knowledge.

To derive the maximum benefits from this chapter, it should be studied, not just casually read. Read and re-read this chapter. Refer to it often and relate the principles contained herein to your every day dealings with people. These principles, if used correctly, can accomplish wonders.

CHAPTER 15

WHERE PROFESSIONALIZATION BEGINS, MEDIOCRITY ENDS

Whatever other changes may have taken place over the past few years, this we know to be true:

The day of the hit-and-run, pie-in-the-sky, suede shoe person is gone forever.

No more gimmicks, gadgets and gizmos now.

The piddler, peddler, pusher, "faker," promise breaker and even procrastinator are things of the past.

This is truly the day of the professional. Over the past decade, the word has taken on a new meaning. At one time it signified limited lines of endeavor such as law, medicine, architecture and similar occupations.

Today the word has a far different meaning. To be professional now has to do more with the quality of one's work performed in a truly ethical climate. A person can be professional in his sales work, his manufacturing, his teaching or his engineering pursuits. In fact, with the increasing demands for quality performance arising from keen competition, actual survival today depends upon a professional standard in all we do.

Today when we speak of a professional baseball player or a professional artist, the idea of top performance immediately flashes across our mind. The difference between a professional and an amateur is not a difference in the FIELD of performance but rather in the QUALITY. The same principle is now becoming apparent in all fields of activity.

PROFESSIONALIZATION DEFIES AGE LIMITATION

I recently attended a huge testimonial dinner in honor of a person who was retiring from a top position in a very large corporation. Never have I attended a fancier function. Pheasant under glass was the entree and champagne was served as though it were going out of style.

Then the speeches started. Eulogies and testimonials began. Everyone felt he must climb the oratorical heights of ecstasy in praise of the person's former record of performance. I almost subconsciously began looking around for the "body." It seemed impossible that anyone still alive could have all of those nice things said about him.

Finally, the honoree was called to the podium and presented with the proverbial gold watch in appreciation for years of service. He was then mentally listed in *Who's Through of America* and finally paroled to his wife and turned out to pasture for the remaining days of his existence.

I felt astounded as I watched the entire performance. The man appeared mature but not old to me. Here was a man whose intelligence had ripened into judgment and whose judgment had finally ripened into wisdom. I still believe that he had just reached his peak with his company.

There is a struggle in industry today between two philosophies. One feels that forced retirement is the only way of providing room for ambitious young men who must have unlimited opportunity if they are to stay with a company. This philosophy is sure that incentive would be destroyed if promotion had to wait for the death of someone higher up in the executive level.

The other philosophy is based on the premise that experience of its personnel is the most vital resource of a company and should be given first consideration. Why, they feel, should they give up a known quality of performance in order to experiment with new talent? Why invest years in a person and then let him go at a period when the investment is paying its highest dividends? Doesn't the company owe a greater allegiance to those who have proved their loyalty longest?

These are the two philosophies which grapple with each other in the economic arena today. I do not intend to champion either or even discuss either any further, although I am sure that advocates of either view could write volumes on the subject.

I am more concerned with the person who is caught between the two philosophies. There must be an answer for him somewhere. He should certainly not be considered a helpless object or a necessary sacrifice to a growing economic trend.

The answer lies in professionalization. The individual today who has reached the professional level of performance has already taken out insurance against a sterile retirement. This does not mean that he can immediately find positions of equal financial opportunity. It does mean, however, that if a person of professional status desires to continue an active or semi-active career, many doors are open to him whether he be forty-five or sixty-five.

The field of consulting is growing rapidly, whether it be in the pickle packing, fertilizing, insurance or electronic lines of endeavor. The average company today has a total of over eight thousand dollars invested in recruiting and training for each salesman it has in the field. An experienced person who does not require any further investment in training, has little trouble securing a part-time or full-time selling job if he so desires, regardless of his age. The executive directors of many trade associations today, holding positions which are steeped in human engineering requirements, are former leaders in industry who retired from their companies. The opportunities are legion to those people who are not satisfied in life with mediocre performance but who attain the professional status. This opportunity does not end with retirement. Professionalization defies age limitations.

MODERN INDUSTRY DEMANDS HIGHER PERFORMANCE

The cost of operating any business today is sky-rocketing. Increased social security and other taxes, higher rent and expenses of every nature demand that a business constantly forge ahead just to stand still.

In order to meet this situation, it is understandable that a higher performance is expected of the individual. Most companies expect a higher caliber of trainee; they expect a person to learn faster and take over responsibilities quicker. Since many companies must expand just to meet increasing overhead, they expect a person to be ready for management at an early date.

Only the person who meets the requirements of a professional can accept this challenge. Mediocrity is frowned upon in all walks of economic life today. This is why the principles of human engineering have become so important. Without an understanding of these principles, no person can ever truly be professional.

IMMEDIATE DECISION

We treat in detail elsewhere in this book the method of making decisions. I want to emphasize, however, that in our fast moving economic society today, to be a professional we must be able, with some degree of accuracy, to make correct decisions immediately. Since the accuracy of a decision can be no better than the volume of reliable information needed as a foundation for our decision, it is important to the professional to keep as well informed on facts as possible at all times.

While the professional realizes the sheer stupidity of giving an ill-considered decision from the top of his head, he also realizes that there are times which call for instant decision right on the spot under both favorable and unfavorable conditions. To lessen chances of a mistake, he tries at all times to have the informational background necessary for an immediate decision.

A PROFESSIONAL IS A WINNER

We know that the word "professional" is akin to the word "winner." Also we know that the words "winner" and "success" are practically synonymous in the thinking of most people. So naturally we think of the successful man, the professional in his field, as one who usually comes out on top.

The professional is a gentleman at all times and has great respect for the rules of the game, but he is a tough competitor and sets his eyes on accomplishing his purpose under all circumstances.

The professional is a good sport but a poor loser in all of his transactions. He hides the fact that he is a poor loser, but it hurts him and the only medicine that can help him overcome this pain and trauma is a quick win in the future. The trouble with being a good loser is that one must lose to prove it. There is nothing disgraceful about being a loser, but it is no honor either.

THE PRO TREATS EACH ACCORDING TO HIS NEEDS

What would you think of a doctor who attempted to look after all of his patients by treating them through a form letter? It would of course be ridiculous. No, he sees his patients, one at a time, and he diagnoses and prescribes for their individual ills. Since they don't all have the same problems, they don't need the same medicine.

And so it is with all who take a professional approach. Anyone who is in the people business knows that all people are different; their tastes are different, their needs are different and they even react differently to the same treatment.

Furthermore, it is normal procedure that in the field of medicine, diagnosis precedes treatment. The doctor does not try to prescribe until he has first discovered the ailment. This same sequence holds true with a professional in any field. He first asks questions to determine the problem involved. Once he has established this problem, he next looks to the solution. Anyone who seeks to present his product or service before establishing a need for it, is not professional in his approach.

PROFESSIONALIZATION NEVER STATIC

We all know that the rapidly changing aspects of our expanding economy and our growing competition call for a much higher type of person in our business world today.

Not only must the person who wants to survive in business today prepare himself just as he would for law, medicine, engineering or architecture, but since he faces new problems and methods his preparation is never complete.

The new field of education and training known as *Continuing Education* is now growing by leaps and bounds. Many colleges and universities have as many enrolled in this branch of their activities as in their regular academic courses.

Continuing education is born of the fact that now it is an accepted truth that a person's education is never complete. A person may be completely knowledgeable in his field today, but unless he keeps abreast of changing problems and solutions, he will soon be relatively uninformed.

Information is accumulating so fast and methods changing so rapidly in some fields, that a textbook printed one year is almost history the next. Some medical schools no longer use textbooks in advanced courses. They would be outmoded almost before the ink is dry.

A new concept in continuing education is that colleges and universities should decentralize in order to provide this opportunity for training. Since those who work cannot leave to attend the classes offered by schools, these schools should bring education to the people. I know of one state university that offers courses in every town larger than ten thousand in population throughout the state.

START YOUR CONTINUING EDUCATION IMMEDIATELY

At one time, the privilege of study and learning was a rare

opportunity. Today any person in any field can carry on continuing education. Fine courses can be taken through mail; others are available through local clinics and seminars. Colleges, universities, and even high schools sponsor educational opportunities which cover practically all areas today. People no longer must search for educational opportunities. Today educational opportunities are searching for people.

Keeping pace with rapid change has its hazards as well as its virtues. It takes much self-discipline to remain stable in a world of revolutionary and radical change. But somewhere between putty-like conformity and radical change, there is a happy medium which leads to the road known as progress. The professional knows that progress is that degree of dissatisfaction with the present which causes us to adopt new and better ways of doing things.

CHAPTER 16

YOU CAN'T HEAT AN OVEN WITH SNOWBALLS

Back in the early twenties a certain speaker came to our small Mississippi town on the Chautauqua Circuit. My father, eager to expose us to the better things of life, always had a season ticket for the entire family for every performance.

I remember very little about this particular speaker or what he said. But he made one remark that has stayed with me throughout the years. I can't even tell you in what sense he used it, but it impressed me so much that I've never forgotten it.

This speaker said, "You can't heat an oven with snowballs."

Over the years I have had occasion to repeat that expression often. It began to have a very definite and special meaning to me. Because of its flexibility, it lends itself to many uses. In fact, I have finally begun to think of this expression as the very foundation of *Motivation* itself.

DON'T PUT OUT MY FIRE

If you walked up to me on the street in an admiring manner and said, "Cavett, where did you get that beautiful suit? You really look like a fashion model in it, fellow," I would beam all over and probably feel two inches taller.

On the other hand if you walked up to me, felt the material and said, "Where did you attend the fire sale? What's the matter, didn't they have your size? Who shines it for you?" How do you think I would feel?

In the first instance you give me the warmth of admiration. In the second you throw snowballs at me.

Let's imagine that I call upon you for a donation to the United Fund.

First, I find out as much as possible about you, what civic club luncheon you attend, your principal hobby, something about the nature of your business and other facts, particularly hoping I will find that we have something in common—a common point of interest.

When I call upon you I have very little trouble striking a responsive note. I know what are your hot buttons, your points of interest. I am able to create the most advantageous climate for an approach. Any preoccupational barrier is immediately overcome. You accept me at once, which is the necessary preliminary act before you will accept my idea or request which I may wish to offer.

On the other hand, let's suppose I never heard of the great principles of human engineering and motivation.

I simply barge into your office, gift card in hand, and ask you if you are the person designated thereon. I know nothing about you and I act as though I cared even less. I am anxious to get the chore over with and simply ask you whether you wish to contribute or whether you don't.

Yes, let's never, never forget that we can't heat an oven with snowballs.

YOU CAN'T HEAT AN OVEN STEALING BENEFITS

I once heard of two candy stores which were located near a grammar school. The first was always flooded with youngsters eager to spend their allowances. The other, although closer to the school, was always practically empty.

One of teachers, curious about the imbalance of business decided to study the situation.

He noted that the storekeeper of the first store would invariably, in weighing the candy on the scales, put less candy on the scales than was purchased and then add piece after piece, to the children's delight, until finally he had the proper amount.

The storekeeper of the second store had the same prices and always gave just as much candy for the same amount of money. The teacher noted, however, that there was a slightly different procedure.

This storekeeper found it easier to put a large handful of candy on the scales and then start taking off a piece at a time. By the time he reached the proper amount the poor kid watching was a nervous wreck. With each piece removed the kid's life became darker and darker.

Was there any wonder that the owner of the first store who was a real human engineer, had all the customers even though the same prices existed? One was always "adding value" and the second was "stealing candy from kids." One was warming the cockles of their little hearts with the fire of motivation; the other was chilling their little hearts with the snowballs of disappointment.

Have you ever realized fully the power of the expression, "Just for good measure"? Do you know the origin of "a baker's dozen"? I'm sure you do. We admire the man who will walk the extra mile. The champ is the fellow who fights an extra round. In the preface of this book we took the stand that it's the "plus factor" that counts. The person who always wants to do a little more than is expected of him is usually the person who eventually goes to the top of the ladder, thereby helping to remove the inevitable congestion at the bottom. It is that EXTRA that heats the oven.

THE OVEN GETS COLD

Every person alive needs to have his batteries of enthusiasm occasionally recharged and the fires of inspiration rekindled. Life, at its best, exacts a toll from us. The human engineer realizes that it's part of the pattern of life to become discouraged at times. Discouragement and failure are not even cousins.

Discouragement is simply a temporary and transitory status that a person finds himself in. Failure is the mental resignation to a permanent condition.

Discouragement, to the human engineer, can be merely the seed for a greater future. It is the clarion call for self-evaluation, rededication to goals and renewed effort. It is simply a cue for taking inventory and a challenge to rise to greater heights. I feel sorry for the person who has never, at one time or other, felt the pangs of discouragement.

Never should anyone feel guilty about finding himself occasionally discouraged. The only disgrace is to be complacent and do nothing about it. No one ever drowns from falling into the water. He drowns only by remaining there.

FUEL TO HEAT THE OVEN

Since we are human engineers, we approach every problem with emphasis on the third dimension, the HOW.

We are not satisfied with knowing that people become discouraged, we are not even satisfied with knowing why they become discouraged. Our primary concern is to know HOW to emerge from a discouraged condition and HOW to prevent intervals of discouragement from occurring any more often than necessary.

If we are to keep the oven hot, we need fuel on hand at all times.

Many people collect bottles or coins; others collect stamps or old wagon wheels. For over thirty years I have kept an inspirational scrapbook. The hobby has now grown into many, many volumes.

When the little tape recorder became feasible, I began transferring from time to time thoughts and ideas to the recorded tape.

I strongly recommend this as one of the most enjoyable and rewarding of all hobbies. It might even grow into something more than a hobby for you.

I have found this hobby of collecting inspirational material and filing it in categories for future reference valuable in two very wonderful ways.

A CONSTANT FUEL SUPPLY

First, I have at all times a reservoir of inspirational material that can perform miracles any time I am the slightest bit discouraged. I can be emotionally at a low ebb and if I put on one of the inspirational tapes and begin eating, digesting and assimilating some of the great spiritual, intellectual and emotional calories that are ours for the asking, I find myself shortly in the clouds. It is such an easy and sure way of pushing back the walls of discouragement and climbing to the mountain tops of happiness.

Through constant pursuit of this method, I have found that it is much easier now to respond to this storehouse of inspirational material and climb out of the depths. In fact, I have now developed the habit of resorting to this material daily just for inspiration and as an insurance against depression. I reach over and flip on the recorder upon awakening. Always I listen while I am shaving. Many times I listen a few minutes before going to sleep.

One of the fringe benefits, also, that you receive from this constant pursuit is that these wonderful thoughts and ideas, collected from the sayings of great people, seep into your subconscious and become a part of YOU. Then your subconscious acts as the old "fireless cooker" did and the oven is heated on stored heat.

Please do yourself the favor of giving this hobby a try. I warn you, however, that if you keep it up for six months it will become a permanent and very wonderful part of your life that you will never let go.

LOOK FOR THE GOOD AND YOU WILL FIND IT

The second great advantage of this hobby is found in this:

In our constant search for inspirational material we form the habit, in all of our reading, our observation and our dealing with other people, of looking beyond the mere monotony of facts, beyond just the doldrums of events, in search of noble living and thinking of the eternal goodness of men. Since we usually find in life those things for which we search, our minds are constantly saturated with positive and constructive thoughts. This is priceless.

I hope you will not consider lightly the constant building of an inspirational scrapbook. I assure you that not only will you always have fuel on hand to heat the oven, but the mere habit you will form of always searching for the good in life will enrich your whole existence, widen your horizons and help you grow.

I GIVE YOU THIS TOAST

If you will embrace this great hobby, I salute you with humility and admiration. Furthermore, I give you this toast with all the sincerity I possess:

"May you always be cursed with the gift of dissatisfaction and divine discontent.

"May you have an unquenchable thirst for knowledge and an appetite for self-improvement that knows no satisfaction.

"May you always be in Grace with your God, in favor with your friends, in harmony with your conscience, yes, even in balance with your banker.

"May you consider each day as a gift to be enjoyed and not as a sentence to be served.

"Above all else may your faith always exceed your fears; no price is too great to go through life unafraid.

"May you think your best, live your noblest, work your hardest and love your fullest.

"And if you will do these things and at the same time master the great human engineering principles, never forgetting that first and foremost you are in the people business—

"Then, my friend, not only will all the good things of this life flow all over you and around you,

"But when you reach the pearly gates, I guarantee that St. Peter will let you enter heaven one half-hour before the devil even knows you are dead. God Bless You!"

CHAPTER 17

WHAT IS YOUR MENTAL DIET?

There is a certain philosophy of life which is a golden thread running through the last twenty centuries.

It started with the statement in the Bible, "As a man thinketh in his heart, so is he." Hundreds of times it has been repeated through the centuries in slightly different words.

"What the mind can conceive and believe, the body can achieve."

"Beware of what you want because you'll get it."

"Our thoughts are the ancestors of our actions."

"Thoughts are the tools that create our environment."

"Our outward actions are only a reflection of our inner thoughts."

There are hundreds upon hundreds of similar quotations which have been handed down from generation to generation. The great lesson is disturbing in its simplicity and yet it is the very foundation of any success which may come into our lives.

WHAT ARE YOU FEEDING YOUR MIND?

Stop this very moment and consider the mental diet which is yours each day. It might be interesting—even amazing in its revelation. How mentally digestive is it? Just what is its quality?

Many people are meticulous to the point of being fanatical about the food they eat. If only they would give the same consideration to the mental food they consume each day, their lives would be far more healthful. Ask yourself just how much planning goes into the selection of your mental diet.

Only an animal puts food into its body on a catch-as-catch-can basis. Most animals just forage or graze along without any planning. Man has developed to that civilized point where much planning goes into his diet. Meals are often planned days in advance. When he sits down in a restaurant, he studies the menu carefully. Books are written and courses of study given on nutrition and proper diet. Even degrees are given in our universities on the subject.

And yet how few people give any studied importance to their mental intake. They give no more planning and selectivity to this than the lowest animal gives to his method of acquiring food. They merely consume all in their pathway as though they were animals grazing in a field.

Just as an experiment, plan your mental diet for one month. Then break it down into weeks and even days. Even resolve that you will become mentally diet conscious and take advantage of delicious mental calories that present themselves sometimes even as a surprise.

I feel a deep compassion for an individual who can't view a beautiful sunset and drink in its beauty and peacefulness with the same enjoyment that he would receive from consuming the most delicious meal.

IS YOURS A BALANCED DIET?

Just as a healthy body must be fed with the proper amounts of proteins, fats and carbohydrates in order to insure a physical health, our mental diet also must be balanced in its contents in order to insure a normal and happy outlook on life.

Do you ever feel strongly that you need a trip, need recreation or need a change? If so, this is not imagination. Just as our bodies cause us at times to crave a certain food which is necessary for a balanced diet, our mental processes give us the signal for a needed change in scenery or environment to cause a more balanced or refreshed mental attitude. We should listen to these signals. We might even call them warnings as their repeated denials can sometimes cause serious results.

Will Rogers once said, "When you feel the urge, don't be afraid to go on a wild goose chase; what do you think geese are for, anyway?"

I have a friend who plans his mental diet as carefully as any woman ever plans the meals for her household. He reads a certain number of books and periodicals over a period of time, some related to his work, others inspirational and still others purely entertaining. Without regimenting his life, still he has certain nights for plays, musicals, movies or other entertainment. He is never too busy to visit with friends, take occasional trips for business or purely for pleasure. These activities serve constantly to revive his enthusiasm and renew his interest in all that concerns him and surrounds him.

EAT, DIGEST AND ASSIMILATE THOUGHTS

Some foods are the basis of a healthy diet and are to be eaten slowly, digested and thoroughly assimilated. On the other hand condiments, relishes and the like are designed primarily for flavor—yes, to make other foods more palatable.

So is it with our mental diet. Much is to be embraced thoroughly and made a part of ourselves. Still other material serves other purposes. Some things are only to be tasted; some simply give flavor; others can even be considered mental vitamin tablets.

Too few people even realize that every thought that enters the mind leaves its residue. The accumulated residue constitutes our subconscious, which reflects itself in our true personality. If we have channeled happy thoughts, beautiful experiences and treasured friendships through our minds our entire personality and attitude reflect these experiences.

Lincoln once said that every person was responsible for his own looks after forty. Since every part of our body replaces itself in a minimum of seven years we can understand this statement. From time immemorial it has been known that we actually create our own expressions over a period of time and even influence our own features from within.

ANALOGY OF PHYSICAL AND MENTAL

If some people eat non-digestible food or over-indulge in food late at night, it is no mystery to them that they toss and turn and find it difficult to sleep that night. Next day they feel tired and are not up to the maximum performance. However, they are not too frustrated because they at least understand the cause of their predicament and resolve that they will take precautions to prevent a recurrence of the incident.

However, these same individuals might have sleepless nights for other reasons. Perhaps they are suffering from anxiety, fear of things to come, disappointment over things that did not happen, petty jealousies and many other mental disturbances. And even though the cause of the sleeplessness is just as apparent, these people remain in utter confusion. They wonder why they couldn't sleep. They don't seem to realize that mental indigestion is far more destructive than physical indigestion—that the mental processes are the nerve center of our very existence.

TRY THIS EXPERIMENT

If you are having trouble sleeping at night, if you are plagued with worries that you cannot dismiss, just try a simple experiment. Set aside one half-hour before you go to bed as a mental conditioning period.

If you love poetry, read poetry—read it with feeling and with relaxation and for the sole purpose of enjoying it. Nothing relaxes the average person more than the spiritual calories to be found in reading the Bible. Many people can condition themselves merely by counting the things for which they should be grateful or even thinking of the good points about those whom they love. In any event these must be positive thoughts and not negative thoughts—you must be strictly on the construction crew and not on the wrecking crew.

Try this experiment for just one week before evaluating its merit. Don't be discouraged if it takes time to master the process. It would be unnatural if you could be entirely successful from the very beginning. Since we are all creatures of habit it would be against nature if a person who was accustomed to reviewing his worries and fears each night could suddenly and without any great self-discipline completely change the complexion of his thinking. However, it will pay some dividends immediately.

THE LAW OF DISPLACEMENT

Your greatest tool in mastering this change-over is found in the law of displacement. It is more powerful when used correctly and practiced constantly than all the tranquilizing pills on the market today.

If I am counting my blessings, can I at the same time be worrying about things that may or may not happen? Never forget the statement of the man in his eighties who said that he had had more troubles during his lifetime than any person he knew, but that nine-tenths of them never happened.

If I am thinking about my loved ones and carefully evaluating their good qualities that make them lovable, can I at the same time be disturbed by envy, jealousy, or resentment?

If I am taking inventory of my wealth of sight, hearing, health, and awareness of being alive, doesn't it stand to reason that some little financial problem becomes dwarfed by comparison?

Sometimes in order to master the great technique of mental and emotional displacement, especially in the early stages, we can find help in repeating certain statements over and over to ourselves.

CHOOSE YOUR OWN STATEMENT FOR DISPLACEMENT

Experiment until you find a statement to which you react strongly. I have found magic in this statement, "May my faith always exceed my fears—no price is too great to go through life unafraid."

Another statement which I have repeated prayerfully thousands of times over the years in the process of mental displacement is this, "May I always think my best, live my noblest, work my hardest and love my fullest. If I do these things I am certain that the blessings of this life will flow all over me."

If you really want this miracle of displacement to enrich your life, you will have no trouble securing the statement which is best for you. Just turn to the book of Psalms or Proverbs in your Bible and read until you find one or two that cause an immediate reaction within yourself—one that you respond to deeply. It is better to choose your own rather than to accept those of someone else unless they appeal to you immensely. If I recall correctly, the first two I ever used years ago were very brief, "God is in his heaven and all is right with the world," and "May Your presence always renew my strength and revive my faith."

Again I say that you should not be discouraged if it takes practice and time to overcome your former habit of carrying your troubles to bed with you. You do not have to be a prisoner of worry and anxiety if you only have the self-discipline to abide by this law of displacement and give yourself a fair trial with it.

BODY AND MIND INTERRELATED

For many, many years the doctrine has been expounded that a person's emotional and mental condition, to a great extent, is only a reflection of his physical condition.

With this as a major premise, a plea was made that we keep our bodies healthy and in a prime condition so that our minds would be alert and our emotions positive. It does not require a psychiatrist with a background of research to tell us that a person who has indulged in excess is in no fit condition the following day to make judicious decisions. He does not view life through rose-colored glasses. Chances are that he experiences some of the disenchantments of life. This law of nature is definite and certain and can be stated without fear of contradiction.

However, let's not forget this corollary which we do not consider as often. Though some may feel that it is complicated, actually it is not. A person's physical condition can be affected in a major way by his mental and emotional condition.

We often hear the expression that a man worried himself to death or that he grieved himself into the grave. While we consider these as mere expressions, they can be much more than that. Worry and anxiety are the cause of many deaths.

CAN YOU COPE WITH TROUBLE?

If you asked a hundred people to tell you what they wanted most of all on this earth, I feel confident that the majority would say they wanted peace and contentment.

Ask this same group just what their definition of peace and contentment is, and you would be amazed at the different answers you would receive. Perhaps most of these would define it as freedom from trouble.

One of the greatest blessings a person can experience in life is the full acceptance of the fact that life will never be free from trouble. A life can never be free from trouble unless it is lived in a vacuum, completely out of contact with people and things. I am sure you agree with me that life under these conditions is not worth living.

BE A CREATOR OF CIRCUMSTANCES— NOT A CREATURE OF CIRCUMSTANCES

Life at its best is simply controlled disturbance—our troubles reduced to manageable proportions. The troubles will always be there; it is up to us to control them rather than have them control us.

All of us are faced with this decision. Our entire lives are to a large degree determined by the choices we make. This is covered fully in another part of the book. Are we creators of circumstances or creatures of circumstances? Do things happen to us or do we happen to things? Do we manage our affairs or do they manage us? Are people our opportunity or are they our frustration? Are we human engineers or are we puppets?

Please, please accept this major premise of life: As long as you are alive you will meet obstacles—you will be faced with adverse conditions. Even the ancient philosopher in the dawn of our civilization warned his people, "The barbarians will always be at the gate."

Life will never be easier—but we can be stronger. Let's adopt a mental diet that will prepare us to accept life's difficulties and cope with them. No life is ever materially affected by what happens to a person or even around a person but only by what happens within a person.

CHAPTER 18

WHAT IS YOUR JOB?

What is your job to you? Is it a means or an end?

The prime ambition of some people is to get a good job—fortunately, to others it is to do a good job. Do you give more dignity and prestige to your job than it can give to you?

It is amazing to find how few people have ever sat down and actually analyzed the relationship between themselves and their jobs. Have you ever known of a person who was elevated to a position of distinction and a friend remarked that he "had it made"? The moment a person considers a job as a destination rather than a journey he has defined his own limitations.

A LADDER OR A ROCKING CHAIR

We've heard the expression so often about climbing the "ladder of success" that, to some of us, its significance is lost in its simplicity.

We know that a ladder is nothing but a tool—just an instrument to use in order to arrive at some destination. Likewise, a job is just a tool to be used in arriving at our goals in life.

Let's scrutinize the ladder for a moment and consider the reason it is symbolic.

First, a ladder is designed for vertical not horizontal use. It is to be used only for an upward climb. If a person is to travel in any other direction, a ladder is not the tool he is looking for.

Also a ladder cannot be climbed except by using one rung at a time. Just as people do not explode into success but grow into it, a ladder offers only a progressive means of travel. We use each rung as a foundation to reach greater heights. If we try to skip a rung, disaster is imminent.

Perhaps the most important similarity between one's job and a ladder is that it requires effort to climb in either case. Nothing can be substituted for this quality.

We can slide down a banister or float down a stream, but the law of gravity makes this downward course impossible if we want to reach the top rung of the ladder. Not all people are willing to make the sacrifice in effort to reach the top of the ladder, but I can't conceive of anyone having so little ambition that he at least doesn't want to go up far enough to remove himself from the congestion at the bottom.

One of the disenchantments of this life is that we do have many people who are even allergic to ladders because of their vertical position. They are content to remain in a rocking chair and enjoy the soothing motion even though they remain stationary.

Recently I was asked to take part in a program through which money was being raised to establish a "Chair in Marketing" at a certain university. For the first time I felt a little distaste for the name "Chair." Do you suppose one would be considered insane or do you think his money would be refused if he offered to endow a "Ladder" in some field of education?

Take a good look at your job. Do you consider it a ladder which you can use to reach the heights of success or is it a rocking chair of security and comfort?

WHAT IS A "PRO?"

As we stressed in an earlier chapter, there was a time years ago when jobs were classified as professional and non-professional, according to the type of work involved. The professional field was very limited in its scope. If you were a doctor, lawyer, teacher, architect or the like, you were looked upon as a professional man.

A whole new concept has now taken place. We repeat that today the word professional or "pro" has more to do with the quality of performance than with the nature of the endeavor. About the greatest compliment which can be paid a person in any line of work is to say that he is a "real pro."

I once heard a person make a very significant remark, which throws light upon the subject of just what makes a person a professional.

Said he, "A society which scorns excellence in plumbing because plumbing is a humble activity, and at the same time, tolerates shoddiness in philosophy because philosophy is an exalted activity, will never have good plumbing nor good philosophy. Neither its pipes nor its theories will hold water."

One of the most professional men I ever knew was a person who had a contract to construct the footings for some houses being built on a certain subdivision. I had an interest in the project and went out almost every day to watch the construction. On one occasion I complimented this man on the way the trench had been dug where the footings were to be poured with cement.

This man beamed proudly and led me to one end of a trench.

As he knelt down he said, "If you'll examine these trenches, you'll find that not one of them is off line as much as one inch."

He then took me to three or four more and asked me to look down each trench.

This man took pride in the quality of his work. With him there was no compromise with mediocrity. This had been the pattern with him in the past, and I am sure it had to be the formula for each project in the future.

Could anyone doubt that this man's work was of a professional quality? I considered him a "real pro."

As we view all great men in history, we find that they all had this one quality in general. None would accept or surrender to anything but personal performance at its best. For instance, if Michaelangelo or Raphael made a slip of the brush, do you think either could walk away and leave it? Do you think either could be satisfied with anything other than perfection in his own eyes?

No, my friend, if you have the gift of dissatisfaction with mediocrity and hold your standards of personal performance high, I say you are a "pro" regardless of what your activity is in life. Furthermore, I assure you that you are already a success, though you may be required to wait for the fruits of success. I even say that you are already wealthy in many respects and that some day you'll even have money to prove it.

DO YOU HAVE A JOB OR DOES YOUR JOB HAVE YOU?

If you ever consider your job as anything more than a tool to use in reaching your goal in life, you are flirting with disaster.

Proper thinking along these lines is very important. For instance, a man who considers his job as an end result which has brought him great security is vulnerable to many disenchantments of this life. He is forever fearful of losing his job. If, to him, a job is a retreat, he has been lulled into a sense of false security and he will too soon realize this.

On the other hand, if a man realizes that his job is just a tool to be used in reaching his ultimate goal and is secondary in importance to reaching this goal, he is not exposed to fears of what might happen.

Even if he loses his job, he still has his destination in view. Fears and obstacles and discouragements are those things we see only when we take our eyes from our goals.

A person who loses his job may become discouraged. But he has never failed until he has abandoned his goal.

A person who is fearful of losing his job does not really have a job—the job has him. He should seek opportunity somewhere else if he cannot overcome this fear. The best way to overcome this fear is to realize that the job is merely a tool. Very often a man loses this tool only to realize that if he does not lose his perspective also he will find an equal tool or one even better. He often finds that by changing tools he loses the fear that he will ever be without tools to use. No price is too great to pay to go through life unafraid.

IS YOUR JOB A HITCHING POST OR A GUIDE POST?

I once heard a man who had made a fortune after sixty say, "A person should retire at fifty, after which the age of achievement should begin."

This man then went on to say that during most of his life a job had been a handicap to him because he had not looked upon it in its right perspective. Rather than thinking of developing and using his qualities to their ultimate, he had thought only in terms of performing those tasks which were expected of him to fulfill his job. He had been chained to his job; it had only been a hitching post to him and not a guide post to direct him to the accomplishment of his dreams and ambitions in this life.

How many people do you know who only reached their full potential in life after they retired? Did you ever try to analyze the situation and determine why this took place?

I'm sure you will find that in most cases it was because they felt emancipated from the burden of just doing a job and finally put their talents into action. They began doing the type of things they loved and *enjoyed doing*. There is a universal law that when a person loves a type of endeavor and gives expression to this affection, the endeavor begins to love him and gives back just as generously.

FALL IN LOVE WITH YOUR WORK

A charming young lady who was an Olympic gold-medal winner was asked the secret of her success.

She smiled gently and humbly and simply said, "Several years ago I fell in love with the water and I think it fell in love with me too. We have a wonderful relationship."

Stop this very moment and ask yourself if you have a love affair with your job. If not, build such a relationship. But remember, the initiative must be taken by you. You will never receive affection until you first give it. The universal law that in giving we receive applies as strongly to your job as to any other facet of this life.

CHAPTER 19

WHERE DO WE GO FROM HERE?

The greatest ambition of anyone who writes a book, makes a speech or composes an article, is the hope that in some small way he may assist in awakening some life or take part in spreading a few truths. Our one gamble with eternity is that we might light some candle that will burn long after we are gone, which may light still another candle, and that such re-influence may carry on forever.

I confess quite frankly that I have a fanatical hope that some of the principles of human engineering and motivation in this book may find a permanent spot in your life. If you will study them carefully and put them into practice, they can be seed upon fertile ground that will blossom and eventually bring abundance to your life. If, on the other hand, they are merely read and given academic treatment, they will fall upon sterile soil and never even take root.

"YOU GOTTA WANTA"

If I had the power to wave some magic wand over your head and immediately increase threefold all the knowledge you possess, or if I had the power through the same wand to give you a fanatical desire to use the knowledge you now possess to the fullest extent, it would not take me ten seconds to make my decision. One of the greatest days of any person's life is the day he captures the desire, or rather is captured by the desire, to realize the full potential of his present knowledge. This book was not designed to increase your present technical knowledge on any subject. It was written in the hope that, through some of the human engineering principles contained herein, you would bring your DO HOW up to your KNOW HOW.

CREATIVE POWER OF DESIRE

This can only be done if you really WANT to do it. Since the dawn of civilization, this desire to succeed or to obtain some definite goal has been the key to accomplishment. The reason is very simple. If the desire is great enough, that desire has a creative quality within itself. It can actually nourish and build into strength all the other qualities that are necessary for reaching this goal. This is not true of any other quality we possess.

So, doesn't it seem clear that if we are to go anywhere in life, we must first have this great belief in something, this desire to reach some goal? I urge you to consider this principle seriously. Please take an inventory of yourself, make a judicious self-analysis to determine just what is your true destination in life. It takes much clear thinking and sound judgment. But this is a great time to start. You are now fortified with the magic tools of human engineering to assist you.

I have never heard this great compulsion within us described more beautifully than in a speech by the late Dr. Frank Gaines: "It is the final satisfying reward of all men's efforts, the sense of building something into a cause, or into an institution, that in itself is noble, that in itself is lasting; and you stand and you look and you say, 'I have been a part of something big, even though I was small. I have done that which shall endure, even though I pass.'"

If there is a spark of divinity or some fragment of eternity that is permitted man during his brief sojourn on this earth, it is the privilege of pursuing with fanaticism a worthy purpose. We can't afford to miss this great opportunity. It is the very foundation for any accomplishment we seek during our life-time.

CONTINUING EFFORT

Once we have embraced this great purpose and brought it into focus with all we do, we still must guard it zealously and constantly rededicate ourselves to it. Never should we feel too discouraged if we lose temporary contact with it. We must have our valleys in order to have our mountains; we must have our disappointments in order to fully appreciate our triumphs.

It will take self discipline and character to keep us in the fixed pattern of our ultimate pursuits. From time to time the temptations will be great and we shall be called upon to rise to our best in order to hold on. Let's constantly remind ourselves that character "is an inner force that enables one to carry out a worthy resolution when the mood in which that resolution was born has passed away."

THE FOUNDATION OF IT ALL

As a final note, I hope it is not even necessary to remind you that while the Six Principles of Human Engineering bring magic to our lives, if we forget other great principles, these six are of no consequence.

Free enterprise, private ownership and our competitive way of doing business always have been, are today and always shall be the three great pillars of democracy. These not only were the initial impulse of democracy but they protected our country in infancy, guarded her in youth, and let's pray that they shall continue to guide her in maturity. These three great pillars are not only the foundation of our country's stability, but they are the only safe pattern upon which we must shape our hope if we expect to survive in this world during the years to come.

THESE THREE PRINCIPLES ARE THE TEST OF A LASTING CIVILIZATION

Every American today should have this great truth written upon his consciousness in letters as big as mountains.

History has verified it, research has certified it, and the years are punctuated with examples of its veracity. The dignity of man, the freedom of life and the worship of God, in all lands and in all ages, have never been any greater than the respect which her people had for the three great pillars of democracy, free enterprise, private ownership and our competitive way of doing business.

Furthermore, no leaders have ever turned a nation Communist, Socialist or Fascist until they have been able to do three things:

Get control of the means of communication so that people are restricted in what they hear and read,

Get control of education so that they can shape the thinking of youth,

And, finally, destroy these three great principles which are the pillars of democracy.

YOU AND I ARE THE TRUSTEES

I once read the following in a letter to the editor of a small paper. Its writer is unknown.

"Our true strength cannot be found in the weapons of war or in our great arsenals of technological advance; instead, it lies deep in our convictions and dedications of the American ideals.

"Freedom's greatest enemies are indifference of spirit, weakness of will, and compromise of principles. This is the stern lesson of history."

Toynbee, our greatest living historian today, could have had this same thought in mind when he said that nineteen out of the last twenty-one civilizations that became extinct, vanished, not because of destruction from without, but because of internal disintegration arising from complacency and indifference of spirit.

Greece has its Acropolis, Egypt has its Pyramids and Rome has its Forum. Let's all hope and pray that some day history will not record the tragic fact that America, too, has only its Statue of Liberty, all memorials of a past civilization which vanished because people just didn't care enough.

THE THREE PILLARS OF DEMOCRACY

You and I today are the greatest exemplars and trustees of these three great sacred principles: free enterprise, private ownership and our competitive way of doing business. And only so long as we fight to protect them will the fires of liberty continue to burn within the great American Heart.

But it's a two-edged sword. When we cease to fight for their preservation, America itself, God forbid, will be holding but short-term lease on simple existence.

We see Communism, mob rule and violence, on one hand, and Democracy, law and order, on the other, grappling as two huge giants in mortal combat to determine which doctrine shall rule the world. If we cling to our great American principles, if we hold to these ideals, then we shall lift civilization to a higher level than we ever dared dream. But, if we ever become complacent and indifferent, democracy itself will vanish from the face of this earth.

United as a people and dedicated to these three great principles, we cannot fail. We are today the only hope of the world, and we will meet this challenge.

Horace Mann said, "Be afraid to die until you have won some great victory for humanity."

Let the preservation of these three great principles be ours.

THE ANSWER LIES WITH US

And so with this though in mind I recently wrote a creed which I titled THE CREED OF THE GREAT AMERICAN:

I am proud of my country.
And I believe in the free enterprise system which made her
    great.
I'm thankful for my sacred heritage.
And I pledge to do all in my power to protect it.
To this end, I don't want just security, I want opportunity.
I don't want to be a kept citizen.

I don't want others to do for me what I can do for myself.

I seek no career in poverty.

I want to earn my pay check, not just collect it.

I want to be able to hope and dream and take chances. Yes, and even fail, and with the nobility of a second start, rise and fight to win.

I know that without this challenge my soul and spirit and all that is within me will shrivel and die.

I'll not sell my birthright for a handout.

I'll not exchange my liberty for a dole.

And this I know above all else:

If I cling to these principles, if I hold to these ideals, then and only then can I stand erect, with head high, marching forward to the music of a greater destiny, facing my flag with good conscience and proudly say "I am an American!"

I believe in my country and her destiny.

I still believe in the original dreams of our founding fathers.

I shall keep faith with my sacred heritage.

I end this book with my favorite little prayer. It is known as THE FISHERMAN'S PRAYER:

God grant that I may live to fish until my dying day,
And when my final cast I've made
And life has slipped away,
I pray that God's great landing net
Will catch me in its sweep;
And in His mercy, God will judge me
Big enough to keep.

For additional information about Napoleon Hill
products please contact the following locations:

Napoleon Hill World Learning Center
Purdue University Calumet
2300 173rd Street
Hammond, IN 46323-2094

Judith Williamson, Director
Uriel "Chino" Martinez, Assistant/Graphic Designer

Telephone: 219-989-3173 or 219-989-3166
email: nhf@calumet.purdue.edu

Napoleon Hill Foundation
University of Virginia-Wise
College Relations Apt. C
1 College Avenue
Wise, VA 24293

Don Green, Executive Director
Annedia Sturgill, Executive Assistant

Telephone: 276-328-6700
email: napoleonhill@uvawise.edu

Website: www.naphill.org